KU-306-430

I AM NOT A
GANGSTER

I AM NOT A
GANGSTER

FIXER. ARMED ROBBER. HITMAN. OBE

BOBBY CUMMINES

FINGAL COUNTY LIBRARIES	
FCL00000453643	
Bertrams	05/06/2014
920CUM	£14.99
LA	

EBURY
PRESS

3 5 7 9 10 8 6 4 2

Published in 2014 by Ebury Press, an imprint of Ebury Publishing
A Random House Group company

Copyright © Robert Cummines 2014

Robert Cummines has asserted his right to be identified as the author of
this Work in accordance with the Copyright, Designs and Patents Act 1988

All rights reserved. No part of this publication may be reproduced, stored in
a retrieval system, or transmitted in any form or by any means, electronic,
mechanical, photocopying, recording or otherwise, without the prior
permission of the copyright owner

This book is a work of non-fiction based on the life, experiences
and recollections of the author. The names of people, places, dates,
sequences or the details of events may have been changed to try to
protect the privacy of others

The Random House Group Limited Reg. No. 954009

Addresses for companies within the Random House Group can be found at
www.randomhouse.co.uk

A CIP catalogue record for this book is available from the British Library

The Random House Group Limited supports the Forest Stewardship
Council® (FSC®), the leading international forest-certification organisation.
Our books carrying the FSC label are printed on FSC®-certified paper.
FSC is the only forest-certification scheme supported by the leading
environmental organisations, including Greenpeace. Our paper procurement
policy can be found at www.randomhouse.co.uk/environment

Printed and bound by CPI Group (UK) Ltd, Croydon, CR0 4YY

ISBN 9780091957834 (hardback)
ISBN 9780091958589 (paperback)

To buy books by your favourite authors and register for offers visit
www.randomhouse.co.uk

CONTENTS

ACKNOWLEDGEMENTS

Charlie Richardson; Fred Dinenage; Kate Beal; Ronnie Richardson; The Open University; Mr Justice Keith; Mike Turner QC; Dexter Dias QC; Juliet Lyon; Colin Cook; Garden Court Chambers; Lord Ramsbotham; Judge John Samuels QC; the patrons of Unlock; Mark Leech; Dr Deborah Cheney; Nick Clegg MP; Edward Garnier MP; Joe, Sharon and Charlotte Baden; David and Ju Smith; Bilal Dunn; Trevor, Anita and William Cox; Queenie, Niki, Laurence Reddy and family; Paul and Carolyn Ferris; Paul Donnelly; Craig Knight; Barry Epstein; Tony Dunn; Chris Lloyd; Professor Shadd Maruna; Mark Oaten; Tony Bull; Andy; Micky and Jack Capper; Lloyd, Chantel, Elka, Yusal, Yukari, Mika and Ma and all those who worked with me on that long road to the OBE.

And special thanks to David Meikle whose flair and enthusiasm helped to tell the story of my life.

DEDICATION

I dedicate this book to my wife, Ami; my daughter, Sophie; my daughter, Abigail, who was tragically taken from us; my son, Kai; and Charlie Richardson, who led me on my path to success.

I also dedicate my book to my friends who have supported me on my journey, and those who are on this journey now. I have tried to show that, even in the depths of despair, there is hope. I see this as a book of hope, and perhaps a guiding light for people who have taken the wrong path in life. I took the wrong path but, with more than a little help from my friends, and total backing from the Open University, I was diverted onto a much better route.

In the hands of the brave, anything is possible.

Bobby Cummines OBE, 2014

FOREWORD

by Dick Hobbs, Professor of Sociology and Director of the Essex University Centre for Criminology

I HAD HEARD about Bobby Cummines decades before I actually met him. In the 1970s any Londoner with an ear to the ground could pick up rumours of violence and skulduggery from an adjacent manor – but only those in the know had any notion of the true extent of an individual's criminal clout.

Working-class London was a cluster of self-contained villages boasting their own distinct occupations, football teams and villains. Local patriotism dominated. For an East Londoner, the three other quadrants of the capital were different, dangerous and ever so slightly exotic. These zones were defined, not by class or ethnicity, but by a familiarity tinged with a sense of difference.

Every neighbourhood had its own villains; theft, robbery and a little light extortion were their crimes of choice. Although drugs were about to dominate the illegal marketplace, this was not organised crime as expressed by Hollywood or the Italian Mafia, but loose networks of criminal entrepreneurs who did not like having to get up in the morning, and would rather risk 'doing a ten' – a decade in jail – than doing a nine-to-five day job.

For a non-insider to hear about villains from another part of London was most unusual. But the name 'Bobby Cummines' wafted in and out of pub conversations, describing an almost mythical presence located somewhere in North London, and associated with unspecified, violent goings-on.

The big marquee names of London's underworld had been buried in the prison system during the 1960s, leaving behind a police force intent on obliterating any family-based neighbourhood crime firm. These were attempting to fill the vacuums left by the Krays and the Richardsons.

This became the golden age of armed robbery. Tight-knit groups of armed bandits, some working in league with corrupt detectives, roamed the streets of London harvesting large bundles of cash from banks, building societies and security vans. And this, along with his claim on a considerable chunk of working-class North London, was why even 'straight-goers' such as myself were hearing the name Cummines.

Many years later I went through a brief period of being asked to appear in some TV documentaries regarding organised crime. On a number of occasions, although we were filmed separately, I appeared on the same programme as a man of similar age to myself, smartly dressed, straight backed, and speaking with an unreconstructed London accent. It could only be Bobby Cummines.

He spoke of a cold, unglamorous world of instrumental violence. He didn't exaggerate, but spoke expertly of a violent and mercenary world with which he was more than familiar. However, I didn't connect this man to the voice that I was hearing at the same time on the BBC, championing the rights of ex-offenders, and who, on one memorable occasion, had hoisted the Home Secretary by his own statistical petard. It took a long time before I connected the violent dynamo of pre-gentrified 1970s Islington to this eloquent advocate of social reform.

As a reformer, Bobby has proved unusually effective, and his willingness to bypass polite liberal sensibilities, albeit with a large dollop of charm, has proved innovative, efficient and, most importantly, successful. Indeed, Bobby will avoid a 'talking shop' like the plague; as a result, he has managed to improve the life chances of some of the UK's most excluded.

Bobby Cummines has been a very violent man. He served a long, hard time in prison, where he enhanced an already formidable reputation for violence and confrontation. He then learned the hard way about making a living in the straight world, with a criminal record hanging over him.

The story that he tells in this book, taking him from working-class London to Buckingham Palace via a solitary cell, is incredible. Be warned: not all of his ideas and opinions will fit with the sensibilities of liberal society. Bobby is a traditionalist, and an unapologetic royalist. But, before the sneering starts, look at what he has achieved, not for himself, but for those at the bottom of the heap, whom he describes as 'our people'.

Bobby Cummines gets things done, and much of his success as a criminal, and now as a campaigner, fundraiser and government advisor, is due to his ability to inspire loyalty in others.

People are proud to be associated with him. I have heard men and women from all sections of British society introduce themselves, or explain their presence at an event, as: 'I am with Bobby.'

This extraordinary book explains why.

Balbriggan
Library
Ph: 8704401

Leabharlanna Fhine Gall

CHAPTER ONE

TO THE MANOR BORN AND BRED

'I've got an idea to make a few quid,' Maltese Tony told me, as our homemade cart ploughed through a muddy crater. It was one of the many blackened pits scarring the landscape after the war.

This particular cart was top of the range for us. We'd nicked the wheels off a pram outside a posh house. We reckoned the family could afford another pram and, as we had no money, it seemed to be a sweet deal.

The cart's chassis was a scaffolding plank, and we sat in a banana box. There was a piece of string on the front so that we could pull the thing around, carrying this and that as we wove a path around the stinking craters.

'We don't need to go to people's houses to get their old newspapers for the fish and chip shop.' Maltese Tony grinned as his plan unfolded. 'There's a much easier way.'

'Let's do it,' I agreed, although still unsure of what Maltese Tony was planning. All of my life I've said 'Let's do it' – it has always been my trademark phrase.

'We can get hold of the same day's papers rather than having to go around looking for old ones,' Tony said, as I reflected on his many imaginative money-making schemes. 'We'll need to get up early tomorrow morning and bunk off school again.'

The next morning we were both up at dawn, waiting for the newspaper van to make its delivery. The job couldn't have been easier: the van driver threw the load of newspapers, all wrapped up, onto the ground outside the newsagent's shop; we loaded them onto our cart and we were off, squelching our way through the knee-deep mud.

We lay low for a few hours, collecting what we could find of value in the craters. When the fish and chip shop opened, we were there with our load of newspapers.

'These are today's papers,' the chip-shop owner hissed. 'I'm not paying for them. You've nicked them from a van or another shop. Both of you can just piss off and don't come back.'

The shop owner, Pat, was a skinny geezer with thinning grey hair. He was from Poland or somewhere like that and I think his actual name was Patryk. He was about forty, I would say, and he didn't like kids. When grown-ups went into his shop to buy fish and chips, they would get the normal amount. When we went in with money to buy chips, he wouldn't give us much of a portion – he short-changed us on the chips.

Well, we were also a bit pissed off, because he still kept the papers to wrap up his fish and chips and he hadn't paid us for our work. We were fed up because the bloke had sussed out that we were conning him; however, we were determined to get our own back.

As we pulled the cart through a bomb site, minus its load of newspapers, we came across a dead cat. It had been there for a long time. All the stuff had come out of its body, but the animal was still furry. To be honest, it looked bloody horrible.

'What are you going to do with that?' Maltese Tony asked, screwing up his face as I held up the smelly, disgusting moggie by the tail.

'Follow me,' I ordered.

Maltese Tony trudged after me with the cart while I marched back to the chip shop. Still holding the cat by its tail, I threw the hairy mass of gunge into the shop. The cat flew through the air, bounced on the counter, and I was shocked to see it land in the fryer, I hadn't intended to throw the fucking thing in along with the fried fish.

'You little bastards!' Polish Pat yelled, hearing the fizzle in the fryer. 'I will get you! I will tell your father. I know who you are. I will have to close my shop. You little bastards. That's what you are. Little bastards.'

That evening, Pat shouted and jumped up and down on our doorstep. He was bellowing at the top of his voice. I stayed in my room as my mum told him that my dad would sort everything out when he came home. Pat hung around for a bit, and reappeared on the doorstep as soon as the breadwinner arrived in the house.

'They threw a dead cat in my fryer,' Polish Pat moaned loudly, bleating in a heavy accent as Dad answered the door. 'My shop has had to close now while we sort this mess out.'

'For a start, you ain't gonna stand there and shout on my doorstep,' Dad snarled, and glared at his angry visitor. 'You stay there, stop shouting, and I'll be back.'

Dad bounded upstairs to hear what I had to say. I told him the whole story, explained about the newspapers and all that, and described the mangy cat incident.

'Robert is wrong and he will stay in his room for a week,' Dad told the fuming Pat. 'You're also wrong, knowing the newspapers were stolen, using them and not paying the kids. I think it's six of one and half a dozen of the other. Now get off my doorstep or I'll knock you off.'

Dad's imposed curfew for the fiasco involving the mangy cat had little effect on my future activities, while Maltese Tony escaped scot-free.

If any boy was born with genes for being a thief, it had to be Maltese Tony. He stole anything, anytime, anywhere. Nowadays they call it kleptomania; Maltese Tony would even raid the shop that sold broken biscuits.

When we went into a Wimpy for a burger and chips he would find something to nick. Usually, it was the sauce in a tomato-shaped canister, and he even took the knives and forks. At school he broke into other kids' lockers and stole their lunches. If he didn't fancy one of the lunches, he would take a bite out of an apple and put it back. It was just to prove that he'd been in there, nicking something.

He was caned by the headmaster for bunking off school. Only Maltese Tony could have come out of the office, freshly caned, and showing off the headmaster's pen; he'd nicked that as well.

He used to walk through Woolworths, nicking the Airfix models. He made a hole in his pocket to put his hand through. He covered it up with his coat and went down the aisle, grabbing whatever he wanted. There were no cameras in those days, so he took loads of stuff and hid it all under the coat.

The end result was that Maltese Tony and I were banned from the fish and chip shop, so other kids had to buy our food for us. We didn't care about that.

The episode summed up my dad perfectly. He was a total 'straight-goer', the same as the rest of my family; I was the wild one. If you told him the truth he would accept it and tell you off. If you told him lies he would give you a proper hiding.

Dad's name was Fred. He was small in stature, but a really muscular man. He had his own building company in the 1950s. He had a lot of lorries with Greeks, Italians and Chinese all working for him. The big mistake Dad made was letting people pay on tick, and he lost a lot of money.

Everything was cash in hand, so the tax people became suspicious and paid us a visit. Dad said: 'Fuck off. What have you ever done for me?'

They didn't like his approach, so he went bankrupt but kept going as a bricklayer. Dad was a proper stonemason and could carve birds or anything from stone or wood. My mum, Mary, preferred the 'warm' wood sculptures, and he had statues all over our garden. She hated the cold feel of the stone ones.

Mum was a little, frail lady with dark brown hair and glasses, and always wore a pinafore. She cooked meals for old people in the street and was always handing out sweets and fruit to kids playing outside. Mum never saw wrong in anyone. She used to say: 'If you can't speak good about anyone, then don't say anything. We all make mistakes, but inside everyone there is an angel.'

Dad and my mum had four boys, including me, and four girls. I appeared on 23 November 1951. The list of children, oldest to youngest, went as follows: Eileen, Fred, Patsy, Pauline, Jack, Frankie, Vera and me. There was a three-year gap between all of us, so by the time I was at secondary school the older children were beginning to leave the family nest at 28 Bemberton Street, near King's Cross. Only Frankie and Fred were to become full members of my firm later on.

Dad made cash from bare-knuckle fighting on Sunday lunchtimes. I never saw any of those scraps, but Dad used to come home with bruises and black eyes and all that. They used to have the fights on the local green. My godfather, Johnny Rattray, was an illegal bookmaker and a great friend of our family. He took all the bets and, after the fights, they came back to one of the local pubs where they shook hands and shared the money out.

We would sit outside on the steps of the pub and they would come out with bags of crisps for us. Our mums would be outside their houses, shelling peas, and they all had a Mackeson stout while they cooked the Sunday dinner. They used to believe the stout was good for iron in the blood.

Then the men would come out of the pub, all pissed, and throw handfuls of coppers in the air. The more pissed they were, the better it was for us, because they would throw even more money in the air.

The drunk men went home to their houses and slept in the afternoon. They would get up at teatime for their dinners. We always had a lovely spread, with fresh vegetables, shrimps, mussels, cockles and all that.

Everyone lived well on Sunday because it was the big day for us. We wore our Sunday best and went into each other's houses. All the adults had even more drinks, and everyone listened to music. We had a lot of music in our house because we had a big piano. There used to be an old rag-and-bone man, Bo, who played the piano and we used to have sing-songs.

If you took Bo old clothes and all that, he would give you a goldfish in a plastic bag. One day he had a huge goldfish and I wanted it. I took my dad's best coat out, gave it to Bo and came home with the massive goldfish.

A few nights later, my dad asked where his coat was because he was due to go on a night out with the boys.

My mum said: 'Robert, where's his nanny goat? You'd better bring that coat back now, or you know what's coming.'

I sniggered when I heard that cockney name for a coat, admitted what I had done, and accepted my telling off. Dad had to go round to Bo's house and hand over two shillings to get the coat back.

My family were pure-bred Cockneys, going back several generations around Islington and Kentish Town. My grandmother on my mother's side was a charlady for a well-to-do family. Her husband, my grandfather of course, was in the Royal Navy during the First World War.

My father's dad joined the army aged only fourteen and won lots of medals during the Boer War in South Africa. My dad's mother was a Romany Gypsy. Her hair was jet black and the men of the time loved her. I heard she was a bit hot and wayward when he went off to war.

With all of that military background we all learned to cook, iron and everything. It was always my job to clean everyone's shoes. I had to clean the soles as well, so that they were completely spotless.

Dad was fascinated by animals and birds. Our terraced house had a big garden and he let a billy-goat run wild in there. The goat wasn't there to provide milk or anything; Dad just bought it for a reason known only to himself. It gave us lots of hassle, chasing everyone all over the place.

We had an outside loo, which meant running the gauntlet with the goat. One day, as I approached the toilet, it charged, and I had to hit it on the head with a shovel. After I'd done my business the goat charged again, and I had to use the shovel on the fucking thing again.

Dad even bought a monkey from a pet shop. It was a destructive thing and it caused havoc in the house. Dad gave the monkey away to a scrap dealer called Corky, who was upset when the bloody thing started biting people.

Dad even had a mynah bird in the house and taught it to talk. We taught it to swear, and it gave everyone dog's abuse. We taught the thing to wolf-whistle and it used to target women in the street on our command.

My family were always fanatical royalists. In our house, the Queen was like the mother of the nation. There was always a photo of her on the wall and we celebrated her birthday. When the Queen came to power not long after I was born, we were taken down to Buckingham Palace to pay our respects and wish her well.

My dad defended the Queen to the hilt and he even had a couple of punch-ups in defence of royalty. I remember when someone insulted the Queen, he attacked them. It wasn't just a slap on the face; he would give you a proper punch on the chin. That was how much the Queen meant to him.

Another huge influence in my family was the Queen Mother. My mum would see how she dressed and, if we were going to a do, my dad would go out and buy a similar outfit – well, the best he could afford. In our family, the Queen Mum had the same respect as the Virgin Mary, she was that important.

The way they saw it was this: some politicians were corrupt, councillors could be dodgy, but the Queen was perfect. She was non-corruptible. You had to look at her as an example and that was how you had to behave.

At Christmas, everything in our house came to a standstill for the Queen's Christmas message. Three o'clock on Christmas Day was the highlight of the year.

There was bomb debris everywhere, even in the 1950s and early 1960s. There were new builds going on all over the place. Everybody needed somewhere to live and so they were building prefabs – you know, those types of cheap, easy-to-build houses.

North London looked like a patchwork quilt. You would have a nice house next to a building being demolished. Those bombed houses were a haven for us kids. We used them as camps, and brought all sorts of stuff into them, using the cart. We turned a tea chest upside down to use as our table and sat on fruit boxes. We collected anything that we found around and about, including bullets and bayonets; everything had a value.

We nicked stuff from cars as well. We had a builder's tool called a centre punch, as it marked out holes for drilling in metal. Well, with that force, we employed it successfully against the rear windows of cars. People weren't so careful in those days, and it was easy to nick things. Once the window was out we could take briefcases, umbrellas or whatever was in there.

It was a battle for survival, with an assortment of scams to provide money for the pictures on Saturday mornings. We used to throw mud at people's windows and then offer to clean them. We even devised a scheme to steal tomatoes and apples from Mrs Rose's back garden.

We had a fishing net, consisting of a cheap cane with a net on the end. We netted what we could, then took the lot to school and sold everything. Mrs Rose was a lovely old woman, but she was never going to eat the hundreds of tomatoes and apples in her garden.

None of the kids in our streets had any money at all, so people like Mrs Rose kept everyone going. Breadwinners who were lucky enough to have jobs received peanuts for their labours; millions of people lived in slums; and I was penniless as well, with Dad having to support eight kids. You have to remember that the famous London Docks were in decline, with other, better-placed British ports taking work away. From the 1960s onwards, 150,000 jobs were lost in the docks and related industries, so child poverty was commonplace.

There were so many characters around. An old woman called Beetroot Annie used to boil up beetroot in a big bathtub. Her hands were always bright red, and you could buy beetroot from her and take it away wrapped in newspaper. Another old lady called Annie with pure white hair did large amounts of washing, including sheets and all that, in a huge tank in her shed. That was their way of making a few bob during those hard times.

We used to collect beer bottles and take them to the local pub to get three pence in old money – a thrupenny bit – for every bottle. The landlord put them out in his back yard, so Maltese Tony would climb over the wall, nick them back and we'd cart them off to the next pub to get another three pence a bottle – for the same bottles.

Some Greek people lived near to us. We used to paint the windows in their houses with black tar. They thought it was still night time and they'd get up late for work. We were paid two bob – and that was a lot in those days – for each window we cleaned off. And it was us who'd painted the windows black in the first place.

We had loads of little rackets going on as kids. It was because we had nothing, and we had to think of ways of earning money. Look at that *Apprentice* programme with Alan Sugar. We would have been well ahead of those people! If he'd given them a hundred quid and gave us a hundred quid, we would have gone out, earned more, and took the hundred quid from all of them!

A family moved in, and they were called the Cherries – their name came from us. They were Italian or Portuguese or something like that, and owned the baker's shop. They used to make Bakewell tarts with little cherries on the top. Their son was always called Cherry. The family were all very religious people, going to church on Sundays. His mum wanted the son to fit in with the street gang to protect him. He was an innocent-looking, vulnerable kid.

'Those kids are naughty, but they're not horrible,' I heard Mrs Cherry tell her old man. 'I think they'll protect him.'

She was right, really. I mean, kids were being bullied at school, but we protected our own as if they were family, although we were just eight or nine years old. If you didn't fit in with the street gang, nobody played with you and you became ostracised; it was as if you were a leper.

A couple of simple souls ran around with us and she saw that they were given complete protection, even in primary school. We didn't discriminate: we went around with a fifteen-year-old girl who wasn't too smart; the older men were trying to get inside her knickers – they took her into the loo in the pub and showed her their willies and tried to get her to do stuff. We told the men to fuck off or we would report them. So they did scarper. The Cherry family saw what we did, and they were happy for their son to join us. We were all ragamuffin kids at the time, and Cherry was as proud as punch to have new pals.

Cherry's mum sent him out with cakes from the shop. My favourite cake was a cream slice, so she used to bring that out to me because I was running the gang. I became the head of the gang because everyone looked to me for ideas and inspiration. I used my organisational skills at an early age. Put me in a group of people and they revolve around me. I was never afraid of anything or anyone, and those qualities always ensured that I was the leader.

One day Cherry met up with me and Maltese Tony. Tony said to me that if we could get hold of lead we would make loads of money. I agreed to take the stuff to Bo, the rag-and-bone man. He was part of the family, really, and always paid a fair price for our odds and ends.

Down at King's Cross station they had an old Victorian overflow system in the public toilets with lead piping coming down to the bowl below. Maltese Tony went into the toilet with a hacksaw and sawed the lead piping off. He sawed about half a dozen of them in the cubicles and put them in our cart.

'Should we be doing this?' Silly Billy asked, clutching his golliwog as if his life depended on it. 'What if someone comes in to use the toilets?'

Silly Billy was one of the simple souls who followed us around. Nowadays he would be identified as having learning difficulties and qualify for some sort of help. In those days we just thought he was a bit on the slow side. He was three or four years older than us, and I remember he went to a special school.

In the 1960s there were no medical terms to describe conditions like his. Today we have Asperger's, autism, dyspraxia and the like. We thought he was retarded in some way, but didn't take the mickey or anything like that. That's where loyalty comes in, from early street gangs through to heavy firms, as you'll find out later.

We just accepted that Silly Billy went around with his golliwog. It was a sort of comfort to him as we went about our daily business. And we never thought it had anything to do with racism or anything like that. There was none of the 'PC' stuff then; if I wanted to buy a tub of jam with a golliwog on it, I bought it, and if Silly Billy wanted to carry his golly around, then he carried it around.

I remember the Robertsons jam with the mascot on – nobody thought anything of it. It was a smiling face and I can't ever remember anyone complaining about it. People used to collect golliwog toys, watches and things like that. The jam company sent out 20 million Golly badges; Silly Billy probably had a large percentage of those, and so did his pals. They were collecting toys, or dolls with smiling, happy faces. To me, what's the difference between golliwogs, Cabbage Patch dolls and Barbie dolls? Load of bollocks, if you ask me.

In our street we had people with all sorts of backgrounds and it meant nothing to us. One of the black kids was nick-named Sambo. Even his old man called him Sambo. The one thing we had in common was that we were all skint. Someone's colour or religion meant zero to us in the early 1960s. Why does it all go so wrong nowadays?

Anyway, with Silly Billy, his golliwog and the gang lurking round the toilets, this guy walked in to use one of the cubicles. He flushed the chain and, instead of coming down into the pan, the water came out like a fucking shower. He was soaked right through and started shouting.

One of our boys jammed a stick in the door so that the guy couldn't get out of the toilet. He was banging on the door, screaming and shouting.

Cherry, who came from that really decent family, was an honest, caring kid and he pulled the stick out of the door.

The guy came out of there like a wild banshee and punched Cherry right in the eye because he thought he was the culprit. The railway police at King's Cross came and saw Cherry with his big black eye – you can imagine the damage, because a grown man had hit him.

Maltese Tony told the police that the guy had been showing his willy to everyone. So they took him away and prosecuted him for assaulting a child and indecent exposure. An innocent guy, going to work, had been showered in his suit and everything – we flogged the lead for £6 and he was carted off by the Old Bill. Cherry's mum gave us all cream cakes for helping her son and telling the police everything.

After that, though, the Cherries had a change of mind. They realised that we were a bit too naughty to hang about with and they moved away from the area.

We grew up around violence and it was no big thing. I remember sitting out on our front doorstep and my mum brought me in because it was late at night. I lay in my bedroom, hearing screaming and all that. It would either be a pimp bashing up a prostitute or gang fights in the street, where they were hitting each other over the heads with broken bottles.

Naughty boys all went around with each other, and that would be the start of proper firms. We went to the same school, had little street gangs and grew up together. Those early gangs and later firms never had any names, really, as we had no intention of giving the police any clues about our illegal operations.

Some kids did thieving, some took up boxing, and it was

a tight-knit little lot. Everything developed naturally. Who could handle himself in a fight? Who was the natural leader? Loyalty was built up in school and it became a real bond. There was no way you would grass on anyone or anything like that.

Gang culture was quite an acceptable thing; violence was acceptable. You learned the laws of the jungle when you were a small kid. I trained the young ones, showing them how to steal things from the backs of lorries, and they soon learned all the tricks of the trade. Maybe I had some sort of charisma, which meant that those young ones watched what I was doing and did the same. That leadership quality stood out, and the kids always turned to me for help and support.

We were all there for each other, and we would never let each other down. It was about bonding while we were growing up. Bonding is a very powerful thing. There is a sense of belonging and a feeling of higher self-esteem.

You were somebody in that gang. You had an identity in that gang. You also had an identity in the manor – the area where you lived. I was 'to the manor born', if you like. All of these early experiences groomed me for life in the cut-throat world of crime, firms, businessmen and gangsters.

There was always a bit of gang warfare to claim some territory. You expanded your territory to operate your rackets. I'm talking about ages as young as ten. When I hear nowadays about ten year olds doing it, I'm not really shocked, because we were doing it then, too, at that age.

As time went on, more and more people came to challenge us. They came at us with sticks and iron bars. So we had to carry better weapons, and we would tool up with weapons like bayonets. Then the other gangs knew we carried bayonets, so they would come looking for us with an axe – then we went after them with an axe.

Members of a childhood gang were totally loyal to one another. Even the weakest link had security wrapped around him. You became a person of importance in your own community, even at such a young age.

That King's Cross area was rife with prostitution, violence and drug dealing. Crime was all around us, and it was natural to become involved in some way.

I went to Grafton Primary School in Holloway, and my secondary school was Holloway School in Camden.

I first became involved in violence at secondary school. On your first day, because you were the new kids, the second year lot ganged up. They used to have pennies in their hankies and cosh you over the head because they thought that was funny. I wasn't having any of it. I waited for my chance and targeted my attackers, one by one. I worked my way through the list and really let them have it.

Jimmy was the school bully. He was the same age as me, about eleven, but he looked like a kid of about thirteen. He was big built like his old man, and had a messy mop of thick, ginger hair. It was quite a spectacular barnet for a young guy. If he saw kids playing, he would take their marbles and grab money off them. He would stick their heads down the toilet, and he weed on the ones he really didn't like.

Jimmy used to meet the girls from the school up the road. He gave them packets of sweets and they let him put his hands down their knickers and all that. And he always smelt of wee. He was a big kid from Connemara in Ireland. I thought that if he ever tried it on with me, I wasn't going to stand for it. Well, we had a fight and I got bashed up really badly.

I went home and my dad said it didn't look like I'd come out on top. Dad had a fearsome reputation as a fighter and I could tell he expected me to follow in his tradition. An image of Jimmy flashed through my mind, and I thought, *'I'm going to get you!'*

I told my sister's boyfriend, who said I should get myself a stick and hit him right across the shins with it. He said, 'With a kid like that, you didn't want to mess about.' He told me that once I had hurt him he wouldn't want to fight me ever again.

I went into my sister's bedroom, because she had a rounders bat. It was like a miniature baseball bat. I put it in my school duffel bag and got up really early in the morning. I felt really good because I knew what I was going to do to him.

I hid at the back of a bike shed that was behind a block of flats on the way to school, as I knew Jimmy was going to be there to meet some girls. I hit him right across the legs with the bat and then I started beating him. I can remember the fear on his face. He was screaming.

I snarled, 'If you ever come near me again, I'll beat the shit out of you and I'll put you in hospital.'

He was crying like a baby and bleeding all over the place. Anyway, I went to school and I was nervous after I'd beat him up. It was the first time I'd done real violence.

Jimmy was in our class and didn't show up for school that day. The headmaster said that he'd been assaulted. The police asked Jimmy who did it and he said it was a couple of big Greek blokes. He didn't grass, and we became friends at once because of that loyalty and respect.

This was really when I discovered that violence pays. I saw other terrified kids wondering if they were going to receive beatings, and I thought to myself that I would sooner take a hiding than have that fear: I couldn't live every day being scared. I built up my inner strength to instil fear in bullies. When I saw that fear in the bully, there would be a rush of power inside my head.

Violence was a method of communication. I suppose I enjoyed it in some ways, because it sorted out problems quickly and gave me satisfaction. When you are giving someone a real beating, and you once feared them, then there is a massive rush of power and nothing quite like it.

It didn't take long before all the parents and kids knew about the savage attack on Jimmy. When I arrived home, my mum said, 'It's terrible. These streets are getting unsafe to walk down these days, with all these foreigners lurking about. You'll have to be careful when you're out and about. These Greeks carry knives.'

The Greeks I knew were diamonds. Their country was in ruins after the German invasion and their own civil war in the 1940s, with millions of people fleeing all over the world. Those conflicts and other periods of strife meant that we were well populated with Greeks, Turks, Cypriots and a whole lot more from that part of the world. Many remained my friends for life. I didn't know too much about their backgrounds – it was all Greek to me.

As teenagers, we went to the same boxing clubs. At the age of fourteen I was Islington schoolboys' boxing champion for three years – I never lost a fight. I was brutal in the ring; I was like a predator going for the kill.

My trainer, Mickey Graham, told Dad: 'Bobby's not going to be a boxer. He doesn't go into the ring to fight people. He goes into the ring to hurt people; he goes into the ring to do damage.'

All of that was true, and it went back to my scrap with Jimmy the bully. I let him have it, and anyone else who crossed me or got in my way met the same fate. When Jimmy beat me up, it had awakened a rage inside me. When I looked at the other boxer, I thought, *I'm going to take you down. No matter what punishment you give me in this ring, I will demolish you.*

For the prizes, there was no 'purse' as such: we received china tea services instead of money for winning. I won so many china tea services that my mum gave them away to our neighbours. Dad came to watch me boxing, but my mum never did as she couldn't stand the violence.

I almost lost an eye because of boxing. They used to put sawdust in the ring to mop up blood, and a chip went into my eye. I had lots of hospital treatment and had to wear an eye patch for years.

Our class at the secondary school was called 4D and no one wanted to teach thugs like us. It was a joke at the time that the 'D' stood for 'Destruction'. One of the teachers was a Jewish woman who knew exactly what we were like. When we arrived for class, she would hold out a wastepaper bin and say: 'OK, boys, throw the weapons in here, please, and you can have them back after the class.'

An Italian guy, Phillip, was the first in our school to get VD, and he was really proud of it. His dad was a pimp. When we were about fourteen, we fantasised about sex, as all boys do. Phillip went with a prostitute and caught VD, then took us into the toilets so that he could show us his discharge. After that, four other kids wanted to go with him to see the prostitute so they could catch VD as well. They thought it was like a badge of honour, but they all ended up at the special clinic.

One of the guys in my class, called Peter, used to nick lorries and drive them to school. What a sight it was seeing this little kid parking a truck, putting on his schoolbag and walking into the playground as if nothing had happened. Like all of us, he was struggling for survival and looking for a way out.

It was the way of life for millions of Londoners down through the ages. Max Bygraves grew up in a two-bedroom council flat with his five siblings, parents and a grandparent in south-east London. His father was a professional flyweight boxer known as Battling Tom Smith. Max's catchphrase, 'I wanna tell you a story,' helped to elevate him from those days of total poverty, and he was awarded an OBE in 1982.

A few miles up the road from me, Roger Daltrey was battling to escape from his poor working-class surroundings. He was born in Hammersmith and grew up in Acton. Daltrey made his first guitar from plywood, and went to school with Pete Townshend and John Entwistle. Roger's magnificent career with The Who propelled him to the CBE in 2006.

It was the same all over the country. Jack Bruce, bass player with the 1960s supergroup Cream, grew up in poverty in a council flat in Glasgow. His mother scrubbed floors in the local hospital. Like me, Jack collected empty bottles to take to the shops for a few pennies. He struck it rich with Cream and bought a Scottish island.

At the same time, the Krays and the Richardsons, all much older than me, were dominating the London crime scene. In the early 1960s I heard rumours that Charlie Richardson and his gang were ruling their manor in South London; I heard that the Kray twins were using more brawn than brains in the East End. I was starting from humble beginnings in the north of the capital.

I was growing up fast. Very fast.

CHAPTER TWO
RAZOR ON THE GROUND

I had heard all about guns, read all about guns and wanted one of my own. I could see into the future and knew that firearms would give me complete control.

My first gun gave me such a power rush. I was only fourteen, still running around in those early gangs, when I heard that a geezer had a Luger pistol for sale. I gave him £20 for it. Even at that age I was nicking things, wheeling and dealing and running little businesses, so £20 was no problem for me.

The gun was so well made with the German engineering and all that. There was a slide that you pulled back to load it, and I could almost smell the stench of death oozing from its barrel. What a thrill to take it to pieces and put it all together again. Big problem: we couldn't get hold of any bullets. I have to say that, had bullets been available, I would have treasured that weapon all my life; I would have used it on every bit of work because I loved the gun so much.

My teenage pals, including Tony the Greek and Andy the Greek, just stared and stared at it. Chrissy, another Greek in our gang, checked out every tiny detail but avoided touching the gun. They were all overawed.

I used to sit in my bedroom, holding the Luger, playing with the trigger and feeling like a god. I looked and looked at the pistol, realising that it had probably been used in the war and shot people. I was fascinated. We gave up trying to get bullets and sold it to a guy up the road who collected gun memorabilia. I asked for £40 and he paid up straight away. I always doubled up my dough.

My fascination with guns grew by the day – I particularly wanted to fire a shotgun. I was just coming up to fifteen when I heard that people were being paid five bob for shooting squirrels. The squirrels were seen as vermin, and the landowner wanted to get rid of as many as possible.

I was a good shot and I loved the feel of the shotgun, and the gunpowder smell. What a sense of power as it kicked against my shoulder! I was in total control, feeling almost as tall as Tony the Greek – all six feet four inches of him – when I saw the squirrels blasted out of the trees.

I left school at sixteen with no qualifications. I was well known as a bad boy and lessons never interested me. I remember our secondary school headmaster went round to see my dad and told him, 'Bobby is highly intelligent, but he's bored. When he reads out his English essays, he stands there and captivates the audience. People swarm around him. But he's just not interested in getting his head down and doing written work. And I know he's running rackets in the school to make money when he should really be studying.'

My dad turned to me and asked, 'Do you want to go to upper school? Do you want to study for your exams or not?'

'No,' I told him firmly. 'I want to get out there and do business. I want to make money.'

And that was that.

I was proud to have my first job as a shipping clerk, just after leaving school, but then I fell foul of the law – big time. One day, I saw police lecturing a group of kids, because a starting pistol had been fired in the local park. I went over and I could see none of them had a pistol; I reckoned that someone else must have fired it. The coppers were in plain clothes. I didn't know who they were, just that they looked aggressive. I told them they were dealing with under-age kids, and they should be talking to the parents or a responsible adult.

One of the CID officers came over to me and snarled, 'You seem to know it all. You're a bit flash, ain't ya? We'll be back.'

I was still chatting to the other kids when, a short while afterwards, both coppers returned and one of them pointed to a gleaming object on the ground.

'You just threw that out of your trouser pocket,' one of them said, accusingly, as he pointed to a cut-throat razor.

I gaped in astonishment. 'You're havin' a laugh, ain't ya?'

'You're nicked, son,' he muttered and carted me off to the nick.

I admit to everything I've done in my life – but not that.

Of course, no one believed me. Dad said the police would never plant evidence, Mum was in tears and the pressure to plead guilty grew every day. Dad believed all policemen were like characters from the old TV series, *Dixon of Dock Green*. He offered to pay the fine, so everything would be forgotten.

The guilty plea changed everything. I went to court and Dad paid the fine of ten bob, or half of an old-fashioned £1. That was a lot of money for us then.

When I returned to work I had to declare my criminal record and was sacked on the spot. Customs and Excise in the port of London, and all other employers, turned their backs on me.

My reaction: 'If they want me to be bad, I'll show them how bad I can be.'

Back shooting more squirrels, and bristling with fury over the razor incident, I thought about my future over and over again.

'Tony, come here a minute,' I shouted to my pal, who was watching me cause mayhem in the trees. 'Why don't we go on an armed robbery?'

Tony the Greek's enormous nose twitched. He blinked several times, glanced around nervously and shook his head. Tony was so tall that I almost had to crane my neck to check out his expression.

'Come on, Tony.' I grimaced as the recoil from the shotgun kicked into my shoulder. 'You want to make a few bob, don't ya?'

'You'll get caught. You'll get caught,' Tony repeated in his usual style, shaking his head at the same time. 'Ba-a-a-a-a-d idea. Ba-a-a-a-a-d idea.'

As it happened, my first job didn't involve the regular members of my gang, who were to become loyal and trusted people in my firm.

I used to go to a club called the Penny Club. It was a teenage venue run by a vicar and you paid a penny to get in. Well, we were in there one night and we saw a group of older guys, about eighteen or nineteen years old.

One of the girls there told me they drove a delivery van 'with loads of money in it'.

'They what?' I asked.

'Yes, I think they collect money from butchers' shops at the end of the day and store it all in money pouches.'

Stan, a Penny Club regular, put his mouth against my ear. 'She said there was loads of money, Bobby. Sounds like an easy job.'

'Let's have it,' I said. 'Let's do it. We need to go off and do some planning.'

We went round to a Greek café in Hercules Street and discussed this bit of work. Stan said he knew that the guys in the club had collected money that day and the robbery would be a piece of cake.

'I'm not convinced,' I told them. 'They're not going to just hand over the money.'

'We've got a shotgun,' Stan whispered, with his pals Mick and John nodding furiously, as if to back up his point.

'Leave all that to me,' I answered. 'You can't mess with guns. I've been out shooting squirrels, so I know how to handle guns. Let's do it.'

We went round to Stan's house. Luckily, his mum and dad were out at the pictures, allowing us to get cracking.

Stan's dad owned a double-barrelled 12-bore shotgun. What we didn't know was that this was quite a rare weapon, worth hundreds and hundreds of pounds. I looked it up and down. We couldn't walk along the street with a full-length shotgun.

'Get a hacksaw,' I ordered. 'We need to cut it down a bit.'

I had no qualms about anything I did. There I was, bang in the firing line, and not giving a fuck. I was the main man, always in control, and had no fears about the consequences of my actions. I really, honestly, had no fear at all. I just followed my instinct, did what I thought was the right thing at the time, and followed it through with the passion of a dedicated criminal mind.

One of the dynamic trio went off to find a hacksaw, and then I went to work, being careful not to leave any untidy ends. If that happens, splinters go all over the place when the gun is fired.

Stan appeared wearing a large overcoat. He looked like a school kid with a freckly face, a mop of messy brown hair and a polo neck that soaked up his dandruff. He looked on in awe as I inspected every inch of the shotgun, loaded it, then gave to him to put it underneath his coat.

Stan had twitched almost as much as Tony the Greek as

I'd checked the gun over. In our language, Stan had stuck up the bit of work, meaning that he offered up the job, but I'd never been involved in any of his escapades before. This was way out of his league, but he came along on the bit of work with Mick and John.

We went back to the Penny Club, hoping to make more than a few pennies.

'Wait for them to come out of the club, hold them up and get the keys for the van,' I ordered as we lurked outside.

'Understood,' the others whispered.

But, as more and more people poured into the club, I could see that problems lay ahead. It was such an amateur job. We weren't even wearing masks, for fuck's sake. Looking back, I can hardly believe how poorly prepared we were. Live and learn, eh?

'Go into the club and pull one of them out,' I told Mick. 'Make sure he has the van keys and we can sort it out.'

Mick went off and reappeared with a terrified-looking geezer. We put him up against the wall and pointed the shotgun at him. To our horror, another load of people started to come out of the club and we had to put ten or more of them up against the wall. John started to unload the van, but we couldn't drive it away or anything with all this going on.

'Don't any of you move or I will shoot,' I warned, full of bravado. I wouldn't have shot anyone – I hadn't entered that league yet – but I had to make them believe that I was serious.

Mick collected all the money pouches and fired up his smoky Lambretta scooter. Stan, John and me ordered the scared-looking bloke and the rest of the crowd to lie on the ground, while we scarpered through the back streets and ended up at Stan's house again.

'We've had a good result here,' I said, catching my breath as we sneaked in the back door.

We explored the pouches one by one. We were stunned to discover that they were all empty: the guys were due to deliver them to the string of shops in the morning. The theory about collecting cash was a load of bollocks.

'Look, there's £6 in here,' John said, as we fumbled through the pathetic mound of empty bags. He was holding a wallet, which he'd nicked from one of the geezers. He'd taken it out of the guy's pocket. That wasn't my scene – I saw petty stuff like that as crimes committed by lowlife. I had much higher ambitions.

'This is a load of shit,' I grunted, feeling disgusted by the failed, hopeless bit of work.

A short time later, as I walked along the street, a police car pulled up. 'We need to talk to you, Mr Cummines.'

People knew us at the club and we were well-known faces. The lack of masks hadn't helped our case. At the police station, there were so many witnesses that I knew we were done for.

They gave us all bail and the next day I decided to tell my real friends – the people in our developing firm – what had happened. We arranged to meet in the Greek café in Hercules Road, where the useless raid had been planned.

How I regretted going off on that unplanned mission with the other kids. The crazy thing was that we had already agreed not to work outside the firm. I had decided what we could and couldn't do. I had broken my own rules. I learned a serious lesson: when you make your own rules, you stick by them.

At that time, I was upgrading from a gang to a proper firm with my pals from my school days. The development from childhood gangs to armed robbers was all about making money. I was in with that crowd so nothing was going to change. We had our own mini-government and ruled ourselves.

We were all at a loose end, really. Everyone was in between jobs; no one could get work because of their criminal records: I had my black mark after the razor incident, and the others had quite a list between them. I just remember thinking: 'Fuck this. If we are going to be labelled as criminals, let's be real criminals.'

I sat glumly in the corner. My brother Frankie was the first to appear.

'What the fuck is going on?' he demanded. 'I've just heard from my old woman that you've been on an armed robbery with a bunch of mugs. What are you doing working with mugs? Why didn't you come to discuss it with us first?'

'It was on the hurry-up,' I pleaded, pointing out that I'd had to make quick decisions.

'You've hurried up to do bird,' Frankie warned. 'You ain't gonna walk away from this. There's a gun involved.'

Andy the Greek arrived and pitched in: 'You forgot the rules. We are all there for each other and we don't bring in outsiders. We would die for each other. We sort everything out ourselves. So what the fuck has gone down here?'

'For fuck's sake, it was a bit of work and there was supposed to be a lot of money in it, so I went for it, OK?'

'Not OK,' Chrissy snarled as he walked in and sat down opposite me. His muscular body and square, manly face looked threatening as he stared me out. 'You're really in the shit now. We've never done an armed robbery before. That's the big league.'

We had plenty of rackets going on, without the need for amateur armed robberies, so I could see his point. Up until then I'd charged people to ensure their property wasn't damaged; moved dodgy gear around; put the right people in touch with the right people; and dabbled generally in low-level crime.

In the early days, firms would have regular business meetings, when boundaries of operations would be agreed. My territory in North London stretched from Highbury Corner to The Archway, across to Finsbury Park and the edge of Caledonian Road. But there were always those who wanted to expand. The Turks and the Greeks at Finsbury Park ran gambling in the cafés and prostitution all over the place. At Highbury the Tong – Chinese Triads – dealt in drugs, but that was usually among their own people. In Kilburn, the Irish firms dealt in building contract protection, and also had collections for the IRA. So you can see that plenty of people wanted to take over our patch and our lucrative businesses.

We had various money-making schemes going – and a lot of them provided income for doing nothing or not very much. My dad, in fact, gave me the inspiration for a really good earner, but he had no idea about it. A shopkeeper had told my dad that his insurance premiums were going through the roof because his windows were smashed by drunks on Friday nights. Kids who threw stones also caused him sleepless nights and the insurance costs went up and up. Well, I asked the shopkeeper about his problems and hit on a top business idea. I sussed that businesses had to pay a fortune after two attacks on their premises – the third claim meant prohibitive insurance premiums. So we arranged for some little horrors to break windows in shops and restaurants ... making sure the owners were receiving their second 'hit'.

We targeted entire streets, and the businessmen were terrified of having windows smashed for a third time. So we then offered to protect all the shops from vandals, made it known we offered value for money, and ensured that future window breakers knew we would go after them. The result: no more vandalism, no more high insurance premiums and a big drop in crime. Sweet!

Of course, one or two shops became complacent and decided to dispense with our services. They reckoned that, with such a huge fall in crime, they could do without us looking after their business interests. Well, we just walked away of course, and, surprisingly, a few bricks crashed through their windows once more. That did the trick, and we started taking their payments again.

Our services also included spreading bad news. One restaurant on our books had serious competition from another eatery, which wasn't paying us. We spread the word throughout the manor that the other place had to be avoided at all costs because of the amount of food poisoning it sent its customers away with. Of course, that restaurant boss saw sense, was allowed to join our scheme, and received a clean bill of health from our 'reviewers'.

I saw myself as a businessman. Even as a teenager, I wore a three-piece suit, and made sure other members of the team did the same. It added an air of respectability and made our operations appear more business-like. We were just businessmen going about our daily jobs.

My suits came from a tiny, thin man called Aubrey Morris – no longer with us, sadly – who was a Jewish tailor at Highbury Corner. He provided made-to-measure two-tone mohair suits. My favourites were a blue suit with a gold fleck and a dazzling champagne and gold version. I also wore a dark blue pinstripe outfit, which I called my 'city suit'.

I didn't pay for those high-class garments. Aubrey was an elderly craftsman who toiled at his cutting table with his skullcap and thick-rimmed glasses, he was an elderly craftsman who toiled at his cutting table; predators found him easy prey. He'd allow hard-up young blokes to pay 'half now, half later', but very often he never received the other half. Some of the punters paid weekly, although that system usually lasted for only two or three weeks. One gang used to take money from his till, then snatched jackets from the rack and scarpered. When he said he was calling the police, they threatened to burn his shop down.

One gloomy December day, planning my next job, I popped in to see Aubrey, and he told me his business woes.

'They're going to ruin me,' he moaned, with a pained expression on his gaunt, lined face. 'I can't keep losing money like this. Anyway, at least I know you'll pay up. What are you looking for?'

'Listen to me, Aubrey,' I replied firmly. 'We can do business.'

'Eh? What sort of business? You don't want me to go robbing, do you?'

'No, not at all,' I assured him. 'Here's the deal.'

'Deal? What deal?' Aubrey blurted out, anxious not to be linked with the crime scene.

'If you give me two suits a month, I'll make sure that no one comes into your shop, robbing. At the end of the month, you give me the list of people who owe you money and I'll collect it for you at no charge. Don't worry – they'll pay up.'

Aubrey grinned and held out his hand. The arrangement worked perfectly. It was a sweet deal, because my top tailor had zero trouble after that. I did knock shit out of some blokes who'd taken him for a ride, and word got round. In fact, Aubrey was so pleased that he took pictures of me in his best suits and placed them in his window.

They advertised me as 'the best-dressed man in Islington'. Can't argue with that.

I also wore the finest hand-made leather shoes from a shop in Holloway Road. The shoe shop manager was having the same issues with shoplifters, and chancers who didn't meet their payments. Aubrey met the manager in the synagogue and told him about our arrangement. I offered the same service to the shoe shop, which was accepted, and I chose a new pair of shoes to match every one of Aubrey's suits. When I arrived for my shoes, the manager packed my old ones in the box for me. He was able to claim on insurance and say shoplifters had made off with the new ones.

As I reflected on those lucrative schemes, Tony the Greek appeared, and said, 'Bobby, you are worth more than this. I thought you were shooting squirrels. Yes, shooting squirrels!'

Andy the Greek stood up and muttered, 'We'll go round to see those guys and make sure they take the rap for this.'

Just as I thought I could escape for a breather, Big Eddie's enormous frame dominated the doorway. He'd been at his bird's house and decided to join in the lecture. Big Eddie was about five years older than me. He came from a large Irish family, with a strict father in charge. Eddie's dad was a big guy and Eddie had inherited that huge Irish frame. He was just enormous as a teenager, with oversized hands and fingers. He used to come to the boxing clubs with me – he was our 'puncher' and, if he clumped you, there was no getting up off the floor. No one messed with

Big Eddie when it came to a fist fight. And for us, he was the complete loyal soldier.

'Bobby, you must be fucking crazy. You know that we don't work with people outside the firm.'

I decided not to make any more excuses. Eddie and the others went off in search of Stan, Mick and John. They found all three and gave them instructions for the court case. Stan, Mick and John agreed to say that they had carried the gun and organised the bit of work. Of course, the gun had been held by me, but their story was accepted; my co-defendants didn't fancy taking on Eddie and his mates. They agreed to say that I was just on the fringes of their operation.

I then plucked up the courage to speak to my mum and dad, who were total straight-goers. Although sixteen or so, I still lived at home occasionally. I had my own flat, but moved between houses; it was important to keep on the move in case anyone was looking for me.

'I'm in a bit of trouble,' I told them.

'What's going on? What sort of trouble?' my mum asked, looking upset.

'I've got involved in something on the street. It's nothing, really.'

When I confessed to everything, she cried her eyes out and pleaded with me not to do any more armed robberies. My dad was no fool and had sussed what had been going on in my life for some time. He just made sure I didn't lie to him.

'I don't know what you do and I don't want to know what you do. But if your mother gets affected by this, we'll fall out big time. I want nothing coming back to your mother's doorstep.'

'I'm doing fuck all, Dad,' I lied.

'I'm not a fool. I haven't just got off the boat. I'm not a fucking idiot. Don't talk to me as if I am a fucking idiot. Remember the rule – it doesn't matter what happens, you will never lie to me.'

I felt a bit sheepish, and probably looked a bit like an apologetic sheep.

'I know you're doing things that ain't right. It's your life, if that's the way you want to go. Just remember this – you've had one taste. In those big prisons they tame lions. Do you understand?'

'Well, they've never tamed a lion like me! And they never will.'

We had to go to the Old Bailey as the charge was none other than possession of a sawn-off shotgun.

I met the Krays for the first time during that court case. They were on trial at the Old Bailey for murder. We were walking along the landing from our cells to go to our separate courts. The twins were in Court 1, so it was a high-profile trial. They strutted along looking like a million dollars, dressed in smarts suits and immaculately groomed. I didn't know who they were at first.

The stockier of the two, with a rounder face, asked, 'What are you doing here?'

'I'm up for possession of a firearm and armed robbery. It was a sawn-off shotgun.'

The startled villain said, 'You cheeky bastard. You've got some front, son. I'll give you 10 out of 10 for that. What age are you?'

'I'm sixteen,' I admitted, feeling so young and inexperienced as I looked at two hardened veterans, who were dressed to kill. Perhaps I shouldn't say 'dressed to kill', but they looked ready to enjoy an evening at the opera. But beneath their lavish garments their faces and whole demeanour gave the impression of serious criminals.

'We'll be seeing a lot of you.' The stocky one grinned as the other nodded.

'Yeah, you probably will,' I said, as they disappeared down the steps to their court.

The screw who was with me said, 'Do you know who you were talking to there? You may not have seen them before, but you'll have heard of them all right.'

'Well, they're obviously villains. Who are they?'

'You were talking to one of the most infamous criminals of all time – Ronnie Kray. Ronnie and Reggie are the kings of the East End.'

I froze. I gulped. The Krays. I'd just talked to the fucking Kray twins. They'd said they would be seeing me again. For fuck's sake.

The sentence in my case, for the bodged armed robbery, ranged from two years to six months; I got away with six months at Aldington detention centre in Kent.

I went there in a well-guarded bus, and as soon as I got off I knew what lay in store. There were prison officers, some in uniform and some in civvies, all over the place. They made me stand in front of a wall and one of them came up and punched me in the mouth. They made me run along a corridor; it was horrendous, as they lined up and beat me as I ran.

As I'd been done for carrying a firearm I was classed as dangerous, and they needed to control and intimidate me. Most of the other guys were inside for stealing cars and all that, so they escaped the worst treatment.

I was taken to a reception centre and locked in a single room. When they bolted the door, it didn't worry me. I was more upset at the beating when I arrived, because that was a million years away from rehabilitating anybody.

I stayed in that room for a couple of weeks while I was assessed. They made sure I wasn't a suicide risk and didn't have mental health issues. They delved into my background and found out all about my previous escapades and the botched armed robbery with the mugs. When they were happy that I'd only done what it said on the tin, I joined twenty-five other lads in one of the dormitories.

More brutality was to come. The 'daddies' of the dorms were allowed to steam into me. These guys were the top dogs who dominated the other prisoners. As they hammered into me the screws just looked on, but I took note of all the faces to make sure they would pay a hefty price.

At that detention centre, I met a black guy called Everton

and discovered that we had a lot in common. We were both junior boxers, and developed a real bond. Everton had also been attacked by the daddy of his dorm, and wasn't too happy about it.

'We should really let them have it,' he snarled over breakfast, as we nursed our wounds.

'Let's do it,' I said, and we both nodded.

I need to explain something. I was short and wiry, but I had great inner strength. It all went back to the fights with Jimmy the school bully. There was something inside me: an animal instinct, a rage within me. I was only five foot six, and there was more fat on a greasy chip (I have the same build to this day). I hadn't known that all this rage and ferocity existed until I beat the shit out of Jimmy.

As Everton and I plotted to get stuck into the daddies of the dorms, I thought to myself: '*I am going to destroy you. I am going to really hurt you. If you hurt me, I won't feel pain. I'm not afraid of anything. You can beat me up if you like, but I will rip you to pieces.*'

Yes, I was ferocious. A bully could be six feet tall. He could give me all the lip he wanted. He could attack me with all his might. But for me, being so small, it was all or nothing. I went at people like a wild animal, and usually won, without any talk or hype. I was ruthless.

After breakfast we walked into one of the dorms and picked out the ones who'd beaten us up. There were several of them, but we fought like tigers, punching and kicking. No one could believe the level of our violence.

The rest of the prisoners looked on in awe as we became the daddies of the dorms. The screws came in and were really sweet to us because they needed us on their side. We could have caused all sorts of problems for them.

Mum and Dad decided not to visit me. It would have broken my mum's heart. The rest of my friends came to see me, though, as I'd expected.

I survived those six months as one of the top dogs, and came out fighting fit and totally brutalised. I'd learned so many lessons. I was ready for a life of organised crime, carefully structured to make money.

I was ready to cause absolute havoc.

CHAPTER THREE
DAYLIGHT ROBBERIES

I emerged from that shithole of a detention centre as a superthug. I'd kept myself fit, running hundreds of laps around the football pitch: if you couldn't complete twenty-five laps at a time they forced you to keep going, carrying a medicine ball.

It was time to concentrate on the business end of crime. I'd learned from my mistakes with the amateur armed robbery, and set about building a professional empire. Those insurance and protection rackets continued, but I raised the stakes to a frightening level.

You eventually get to a stage, when violence escalates, where you become like a god, deciding who lives and who dies. In practical terms, my tactics became a means to an end. If someone was interfering with my business, I 'educated' them by telling them that they were in danger. If that didn't work they were intimated: put up against a wall and a gun smashed in their mouth. If they still didn't listen, and they continued to operate business in an unacceptable way, they were eliminated. I call that the eternal triangle of violence: education, intimidation and elimination.

I depended on reliable information, a detailed plan, the right people to carry it out and the right tools for the job.

Every day people get up to go to work, climb aboard the bus with the same people, talk about what happened the night before and moan about their workload. They talk about their boss being a creep, or discuss their debts and the kids. For years and years they go to work like bees working for the queen bee.

Management at the top of the tree exploit the average person, and there is no way out. When you're trapped with a mortgage and a family to clothe and feed, there is no escape. They are slaves to industry, with the promise of a few weeks' holiday in the sun in some shithole in Spain or Greece. There, they are ripped off by the locals and come home with dodgy trinkets, the type you might see in the local cut-price, rubbish shop.

Armed robbers, operating as businessmen, have a completely different life. On the other hand, gangsters charge around like bulls in china shops, causing chaos, drawing attention to themselves and giving everyone a bad name.

I'll tell you how a real professional armed robber operates. These people enjoy the high life for short periods, then are caught and banged up in a concrete tomb for longer periods. They sleep next to the toilet and practise the art of chronic masturbation, dreaming of the women they've been with. They believe that it is better to live the high life for dazzling short periods than to endure a life of drudgery.

Armed robberies are not done on the spur of the moment. Only muggers do that, so you can see why they are called muggers. The wise guys rob the banks and get the big money. The muggers rob people in the street and get small money. Both get similar sentences when caught; muggers really are mugs.

We got up at the same time as our neighbours, but that was where the similarities ended. We went to a café to have a full English breakfast, and met the rest of the firm to look at possible jobs. It was important to have a normal routine; we didn't want anyone to ask questions or get suspicious. The worst thing in the world was suspicious neighbours. Those who knew me and grew up with me kept their mouths shut, for fear of retribution.

People in my street thought that I was a kind, polite, happy-go-lucky guy who worked in an office in a well-paid job in the city. People in the city had yet to hear about my desire to relieve them of their billions. A genuine city job would have come my way, but for the 'razor on the ground' incident.

I remember walking to the café to plan a bit of work, the sun shining on my face and feeling good. Inside I would smell the bacon, sausages and eggs being fried and hear the guys from the building sites discussing football. Most of them were just having a right laugh.

The pimps and prostitutes appeared after their night's work, usually arguing over money. Next came the elderly people, ready to do their shopping, while we sat there reading the newspapers and eating our breakfasts. We all tucked in, with Old Frank the driver and Neil, one of our other wheel men – getaway drivers – gorging themselves on extra help-ings of bacon and fried bread. I had my full English spread with black Turkish coffee to boost my energy levels.

Old Frank was a lovely guy, about twenty years older than me, in between the ages of my dad and older brother, Freddy. He was trying to hold on to his black hair, despite bald bits appearing here and there.

I bumped into Old Frank because I was friendly with his young son, Alan. Old Frank was Irish, and his family were all solid people. I went round to their house one day for some Irish stew and they were keen to know what I did for a living.

'You and your mates seem to be doing really well,' Old Frank had said, 'but I'm not bringing in many readies at the moment.'

'What are you doing?' I'd asked, seeing the potential.

'I'm driving cars and cabs, and that's about it,' Old Frank had mumbled in reply. 'What are you up to?'

'We rob banks and run a few businesses,' I'd answered, proud of my operations. 'My brother Frankie is involved in another side of the business now, so would you like to drive for me?'

He'd gaped. 'I knew you were a bad boy, but not that bad!'

'Only thing is, you have to be round my house early every morning, suited and booted.'

'I don't have a suit,' Old Frank answered, looking down-cast.

We went out and bought an expensive suit. Problem solved, and Old Frank looked the part. 'Fucking hell, I've never worn a suit like this! Don't know if I've even seen a suit like this!'

Old Frank became totally loyal to me and fitted into my firm like a dream.

Neil was a painter and decorator and I met him through a girlfriend. We were talking one day over a beer and he said he needed to earn some money, as painting and decorating wasn't earning much dough.

He looked a solid guy, so I asked, 'What about you driving for us?'

'What, delivering parcels?'

'Well, not exactly.' I laughed. 'We do more ... collecting, if you like.'

'I'm not with you.'

'OK. Come down to the Enkel Arms tomorrow morning and I'll show you what business we're in.'

I met him outside the pub, having collected some weapons from their hiding places. Neil looked shocked. 'Oh, fucking hell, I'm not in the IRA!'

'No, no, we're not a terrorist organisation. We're into looking after people who are getting fucked about. We make sure people aren't intimidated. And you'll find that we go out on a bit of work now and again.'

Neil gaped at a sawn-off shotgun. He was frozen to the spot.

'How much are you earning?' I asked, watching him like a hawk for any sign of weakness.

'I'm not,' he grumbled.

'Come out with me and you will get £250 a week, every week. But if you rat on us there is a problem.'

'A problem?'

'If you rat on us, I will shoot you.'

We shook hands and Neil became a loyal and trusted member of the firm, and a top-class driver.

After the café emptied, we'd sit and talk about what was on our special menu for the day. The starter was the planning, the main course was the robbery itself and the dessert was the reward of loads of cash. We studied the various bits of information that had been passed on to us: we went through them all in the finest detail, and selected the best jobs.

The 'paid for' information coming in was vital because it dictated how much we could earn. For example, a betting shop might only have a couple of grand at the start of the day, but there were rich pickings at the end of a good day: Friday and Saturday were the ideal times after all the punters had had their weekly pay. Monday was normally a dead day, because the punters would have blown their wages over the weekend.

Timing and inside knowledge were key. The best form of information came from a disgruntled employee who had worked for the bookie in the past and knew the staff's routines. We loved the bosses who treated their workers like shit; they were the ones who would help to set up a robbery. During a robbery, when the bosses were lying on the floor, we'd give them a kick in the ribs on the way out, because it brought a smirk to the faces of the rest of the disgruntled staff.

Once the target had been chosen, we would get into our cars and go for a viewing, like newlyweds checking out their first home. We went all over London to wherever there was a bit of work. That could be on our own territory or anywhere in the capital. We'd look at the building, and one of us would go inside on the pretence of looking for a job. They'd always keep our man waiting to see the person in charge, before he was eventually taken to the office, so that time was used to check the layout of the building, how many staff were around, where everyone sat, and where the alarm buttons were placed.

After that, we would survey the surrounding areas for our getaway. That was the most important part of the job. Every robbery was planned around the getaway, because it was no use stealing all the cash, only to be nicked trying to flee from the scene. Quite a few robbers have been nicked because they didn't plan the getaway properly, or they left loose ends. The Great Train Robbery was an example of that. Clues were left behind in a barn, and that cost them thirty years in jail time. The robbery was planned and executed with perfection, but the clearing up after the event was sloppy.

In this day and age, nothing has changed: the getaway and clearing up for the modern-day criminal have to be done to the same standard as the robbery itself. But we all know that, in moments of jubilation, we forget. Contrary to popular belief, the Old Bill aren't stupid. Their mob is just as good as your mob. They have the best equipment money can buy, they think like armed robbers and have intelligence on every villain who's 'at it'. If you underestimate them, you will be doing big porridge, as 85,000 prisoners doing a bit of bird today will tell you. Every one of them thought that they could beat the police. Number one rule: always respect the capabilities of the Old Bill.

Back in our day, once all the escape routes had been decided, the armed robber continued planning the bit of work. It was decided who would be the driver and who would act as back-up – it was always safer to have two drivers who knew the escape routes in case one fell sick or we needed to swap cars.

The day before the robbery was due to take place we would say goodbye to our loved ones, telling them we would be away for a few days visiting friends. We'd then all meet up at a pre-arranged rendezvous. We normally used the flat of a friend. We would pay him to go on a two-week holiday, with a few quid on top if the work was successful. Old Frank brought the guns from his secret hiding place, along with masks and clothing. We wore boiler suits and crash helmets for the heavy jobs. The helmets protected our identities, and would help keep our heads intact if anyone tackled us.

We would lay the guns and ammunition out on the bed and check them over. Old Frank would check out both the cars and drop one off at a pre-arranged spot for the change-over after the robbery. Next, he would make his way back to the pad by public transport. He never used a cab, as that could be used to trace an address.

On the way to the pad, Old Frank would pick up meals from the local takeaway and we'd usually watch a bit of television. We'd talk, then bed down for the night. There was no alcohol, drugs or anything, because everyone had to be on top form in the morning. Each of us slept with his own thoughts about the job and our families. I would go over the robbery time and time again in my head until I fell asleep.

Old Frank was always the first one up because he wanted breakfast. One of the firm would stay behind with the guns while we headed off to the café in Hercules Road. We never spoke at the café on the day of the work; we had breakfast, read the papers and went back to the pad. We'd take a breakfast sandwich back to whoever was staying behind with the guns.

One particular robbery that I remember, Chrissy was nominated to babysit the pad and our personal effects. I was to be lead gunman, with a sawn-off shotgun called Kennedy: we'd named it after the assassinated American president.

Kennedy had begun life as a fully-fledged .410 bore shotgun, used for shooting rabbits, squirrels, birds or whatever. That size means the bore of the barrel was .410 of an inch. Kennedy's butt had been replaced with a pistol grip and, of course, the barrel was sawn off. It looked menacing, with double hammers and two triggers. The weapon was easy to conceal under an overcoat, and the sawn-off barrels meant a much wider spread for the pellets.

A professional gunsmith, on my payroll, had carried out some clever work on it. I put plenty of business his way and he looked after the tools of my trade. I was careful to use my professional man: amateur modifications usually resulted in the bloody thing blowing up in your face. I'd heard of robbers becoming brown bread (as we always said, instead of 'dead'), with their brains blown out in a flash after a shoddy repair job.

Kennedy could cause havoc in a crowded bar. The full-size original version would have taken out two or three people, but the modified Kennedy – resembling a pirate's pistol – had the potential of taking out an entire group because of that wide spread. Let's say it excelled in crowd control.

Kennedy also made the loudest bang you were ever likely to hear and the room would be enveloped in an acrid, sulphur-type smell. Your mouth and nose filled up with the overpowering fug of Guy Fawkes Night thanks to a strong whiff of gunpowder. In Kennedy's case, there were no bonfire night frolics; he dealt in life and death, and could snuff out someone's existence with a flick of his trigger.

My brother Frankie was the other gunman on many jobs, and he had a revolver. Neil was the bag man, who'd scoop up the loot. Old Frank would take care of the transport.

We picked up our lethal tools and put them under our coats, with our masks in our pockets. We all had £40 on us, in two £20 notes, in case things went wrong and we had to split up. We had nothing else – no ID or anything – just the tools and the £40 each.

We walked down the stairs of the pad and got into the car. Once we walked out of that house onto the street with shooters, there was no turning back.

The gunmen always sat in the back of the car. There was no real reason for that, apart from being part of a strict routine where everyone knew their role down to the finest detail.

We drove along quietly, obeying the speed limits and not doing anything that would draw attention to us. We had no intention of getting nicked before going on the bit of work. Can you imagine having to live that down?

I could feel Kennedy nestled snugly against my chest, close to my heart. It was like a babe in arms – this tool was my protector – and you had to respect it and look after it. Kennedy would do the same for you.

Old Frank stopped the car and checked his mirrors to make sure all was clear. Then he went through his little ritual, with the words, 'Gentlemen, are you ready?'

Next, my words, that everyone wanted to hear, especially Old Frank, who said my catchphrase really gave him a buzz: 'Let's do it!'

We were out of the motor and into the building in a flash. 'Everyone on the floor!' we screamed out.

If any of the staff weren't moving fast enough or hesitating to obey the command, we fired a shot into the ceiling.

That always sorted out the problem. The sound of a gunshot and the smell of burning gunpowder always brought everyone into line. We had three minutes to finish the work before the police arrived. The last thing you wanted was the Old Bill on your case.

Neil knew where all the money was because of the inside information. He moved like a sprinter, scooping it all up and thrusting it into his bag. He loved doing that – he said it made him feel like Father Christmas with his sack of presents for the guys.

When the job was complete, my brother Frankie was the first one out of the door with the hand gun, making sure that the bag man got into the car safely. I was the last one out, keeping the staff under control.

We all piled into the car and made for the change-over spot. We transferred the guns, masks and everything into the other motor, changed clothes in a jiffy, and Old Frank drove off alone. The car used for the raid was then parked up. It had been 'acquired', with no links to any of us, so we were in the clear there.

The rest of us split up and made our own way back. Neil now had the money in a holdall, along with a spirit level, on view, so that he looked like a building-site worker. My brother Frankie and I were dressed smartly to fit in with the crowds on the street.

What a relief to arrive back at the pad. Old Frank had already hidden the guns, disposed of our work clothes and parked the change-over car in a side street. We sat down to count the takings, letting Chrissy do most of that so he didn't feel left out. He was keen to hear all about the bit of work, so we gave him the main details.

One of the boys went out to get some booze, plus bitter lemon for me, and we sat and divided the money into equal shares. I always stuck to bitter lemon, because my concentration levels had to be 100 per cent, twenty-four hours a day. I'd seen people making mistakes after drinking, and I vowed that would never happen to me.

I had a rule that everyone received the same amount, even if they were just minding the pad. That way no one became jealous or thought they were hard done by. They also had no reason to grass, because they got an equal amount for the bit of work. We didn't ever bother reading up about it all in the papers the next day. For a start, the people who'd been robbed always multiplied their losses – but we knew exactly how much had been taken!

Armed robberies don't always go to plan, however. I remember on two occasions when they went terribly wrong. I cringe when I think about the first bodged job.

Black Jerry came up to us one night in the pub, and said he had a bit of work that was too big for him but might suit us – Jerry was a shit-hot shoplifter, but wasn't really into the heavy stuff. He said the guy who'd told him about the job – we called them spotters – said there were easy pickings from a van carrying wages for a building site. Apparently the foreman and a labourer went to collect the cash from the bank in the firm's van. The labourer was tooled up with a pickaxe handle and the foreman carried the money bag.

We arranged to meet the spotter and did our best to check out his information, to see what kind of money was paid out at the site on pay day. We decided to give him the benefit of the doubt, gave him a grand up front and went on the bit of work.

As we pulled up in a side street near the bank, we saw the foreman and labourer get out of their van and go into the bank. Then they reappeared, obviously carrying a bag full of cash.

As I put my crash helmet on, slid down the visor and hurried out of the car with Kennedy, to my horror I noticed another guy getting out of a car, also masked and tooled up with a shotgun.

He looked at me, I looked at him and we both thought: *'What the fuck is going on here?'* I knew he wasn't Old Bill and he knew I wasn't Old Bill, either.

While we checked each other out, the foreman and driver made a break for it. We both clambered into our cars and pulled off in different directions,

'What the fuck was all that about?' Old Frank asked, looking confused, as we drove off.

'Haven't a clue,' I answered, just as confused. 'That other firm was after the same prize as us, so someone has a lot to answer for. I bet the spotter sold the job to two firms and collected a grand from both of us.'

Well, we looked for him, but he had rapidly fucked off the

manor with his two grand. We found out later that the other firm on that bit of work came from the East End. We had a laugh with them about it. Black Jerry was embarrassed about the whole thing, but it wasn't his fault. We swore that if we ever met the little informant bastard again, we would string him up by his bollocks. And we would have done just that.

The other incident was much more serious. We went on a bit of work, scooped up the money, and chose a route over the River Thames on the return journey. I lay in the back, as usual, with the shotgun across my chest. All of a sudden I smelled shit. I checked my shoes but could see nothing.

'Which one of you has trod in dog shit?' I muttered.

'It's him,' Old Frank said accusingly, pointing at Dave, who was an enormous guy and handy in a ruck.

'Take your fucking shoe off and hang it out the window,' I told Dave. 'It's stinking the car out and making me feel sick. I can't stand bad smells.'

'It's not his shoes,' Old Frank whispered. 'He shit his pants on the bit of work.'

'Is that right?' I asked, hardly believing what I was hearing.

Dave looked at me and then looked at the floor of the car. He was shaking, with a regular flow of tears rolling down his cheeks.

'That's what happened,' the giant of a man said. 'I've never been on an armed robbery before and I did just shit myself.'

Old Frank and I exchanged glances via the driver's mirror. It was my job to explain everything to Dave.

'If you're like this on a bit of work, what will you be like if the Old Bill pulls you in for questioning? They're giving armed robbers thirty years inside these days.'

'Bobby, I would never grass any of you lot up,' Dave pleaded through a flood of tears.

'I know that,' I told him. 'I'm just glad the bit of work wasn't as shitty as the smell. Frank, stop the car when we get to the bridge so that me and Dave can get some fresh air. We'll get some fresh air into the car as well.'

Old Frank wasn't stupid. He knew what was going through my mind. Dave was a liability. The best option was to shoot him and dump him over the bridge.

Yes, for me to be considering that option was an enormous escalation in violence. But that is the way I was thinking; it wasn't just bravado. As I told Dave, captured armed robbers were going away for a very long time. I saw that the only way out of our predicament was to dispose of our passenger. I would have done so with no regrets.

'I can't stop here – there's too much traffic about,' Old Frank grumbled as the Thames came into view. 'Let's wait and sort it out when we get home.'

That mug owed his life to Old Frank that night. Dave was so very nearly brown bread.

When we arrived back at the pad I told Dave to go to the bathroom and clean himself up. While he was gone, I looked at Old Frank; he knew I could have done that bit of work – the traffic wasn't too bad.

Old Frank told me straight: 'I knew what you were

thinking, but it was a crazy idea. If you topped him you'd get too much bird. I mean, he's been on that bit of work with us and played an active part, so he can't scream "Coppers!" He's in it up to his neck.'

When Dave returned from his shit-cleaning exercise, I told Old Frank to share out the money in equal amounts as usual.

'I don't want any,' Dave said, as the mounds of cash appeared on the table. 'You guys keep it all, because I fucked up.'

'No, you'll take your share,' I commanded. 'You took the same risks, and if we get nicked you will get the same amount of jail time.'

We knew that the more involved Dave became, the less likely he was to spill the beans. We made him take his money to ensure he was heavily involved in the crime.

Dave looked sheepish – although now at least he didn't smell like one – and left as quickly as he could. Maybe he realised he had been within an inch of his life a few hours earlier and owed his survival to Old Frank.

'We'll have to keep an eye on him for a while,' was all I said.

Old Frank nodded, with that wise look that only years of experience can bring.

Valuable lesson learned: just because a guy is big built, and can have a ruck in a pub, doesn't mean that he can be an armed robber or a gunman willing to kill. The really dangerous men I've worked with have always been small to medium build – don't forget that I am tiny and wiry. The Krays, Frankie Fraser and Charlie Richardson were not exactly giants in the physical sense, but they were not the type of people you would want as enemies. They killed if they had to.

Needless to say, Dave never went on any more armed robberies. I heard that he tried the armed robbery game for a while afterwards, got nicked and gave evidence against his co-defendants. He never said a word about our firm.

I suppose that being a known grass is one thing; being a grass who shits himself on a bit of work is a bridge too far, even for people like Dave.

CHAPTER FOUR
THE STINGER

Tony the Greek, still one of my best pals during the crazy time after the detention centre, was a worried man. I'd never seen anyone look so worried. His face was in total panic mode, with regular twitches controlling his eyes and mouth. He clenched and unclenched his fists, waved his arms around, then sat down and stood up. After more hand waving, he sat down again and continued to twitch.

'Bobby, Bobby,' he blurted out, as I'd walked into the Enkel Arms. 'I've got bad news. B-a-a-a-d news.'

'Calm down, calm down,' I told him, realising I'd picked up his annoying habit of saying everything twice. Not only that, when he worked himself up into a proper lather, he'd say, 'Oooo oooo.' I was used to it, but others were not so forgiving.

'Bad news, b-a-a-a-d news. Oooo oooo!'

Tony the Greek, all the way through from his school days, had dabbled in petty crime. He was always on the fringe of heavy stuff, but never quite made the grade. He would nick this and that, sell on some stolen carpets and offer round a bit of puff. He was a regular sight with a box of watches, an armful of kettles, a pile of plates or anything else he could lay his hands on. He'd never been on any proper work; we didn't ask him to go, and we couldn't imagine him at the sharp end.

Because I'd grown up with Tony the Greek, I knew his habits off by heart. In football terms, he would have been a product of the youth system who never quite made it. He was always on the fringes of the first team, but lacked the talent and imagination to make the grade. He wasn't the type you would want beside you in the trenches, waving his arms around and causing mayhem right, left and centre.

On the other hand, Tony was as good as gold. He was ten years older than me and would lay his life on the line for his friends. I just wished he would act and talk normally.

'Bobby, Bobby, oooo oooo!' he continued, to the annoyance of my brother Frankie, Eddie the mountainous minder and driver Neil, as we sat in a side room to discuss business arrangements.

'What's it all about, Tony?' I pleaded as he jabbered and waved his arms about, threatening glasses and bottles all around us.

'Your mum knows these people. Your mum knows these people.'

My ears pricked up. My mum and dad had endured the 'razor on the ground' stuff and the detention centre episodes, and were really dear to us all. So if he said 'your mum and dad know them', we would have to listen and do something about it.

'What people?'

'Ooooo. Ooooo. Stavros and Eva. Stavros and Eva.'

We all leaned forward and listened.

'You know, it's the fish and chip shop not far from your mum's house,' Tony explained, as I sat nursing a bitter lemon in the quiet room beside the busy bar. 'They're a nice little family. They're good people. They'll be having a break-down soon. They'll be having a breakdown soon.'

I wondered what had happened to Stavros and Eva. Now and again we would pop in to their shop if somebody fancied a bag of fish and chips, but most of the time we ate in restaurants like the Greek ones, or the Indian or Chinese. We used to go out for meals because we had money.

Stavros and Eva knew me from when I was a young boy growing up – I used to say hello to them. They were a nice family; they were nice people. My mum and dad used to chat to them because they were around about the same age.

'What's going on?' I asked, trying to move Tony on to his main point. He was so on edge that he twitched and shook like a nervous rabbit. He paced around the bar and returned, ready to provide another instalment about the chip shop family's predicament. He also returned with another bitter lemon for me.

'It's bad news,' Tony blurted out, talking fast and drinking at the same pace. 'Their daughter has got caught up with some Turkish guys. Turkish guys.'

Tony was an unmistakable figure in the Enkel Arms. The pub in Holloway was usually packed with Irish revellers, but he towered above everyone. His thick black hair was curly, he had a large nose and, basically, he stood out in a crowd.

Tony was over the top with birds; Tony was romantic. If he chatted up a girl, he would buy her a drink – then disappear off to get her a flower. Sometimes he would run off and come back with a box of chocolates. He was over the top with everything. If he bought you a drink, he would buy everyone in your company a drink, too. He was very generous in that way.

'Spit it out, Tony,' I urged him, keen to know what the Turks were up to.

'These guys have their daughter on heroin. And now they're trying to get her on the game. Can you sort it? Stavros and Eva will pay whatever you want.'

Well, I wasn't worried about being paid. I'd just been out on a nice little earner, robbing, so it was a case of keeping everything sweet in the manor. We'd been trouble-free for a while. I could see that my services were needed sharpish, though.

'Bad news, bad news,' Tony muttered, turning to Peter the Poof, who'd strolled in a bit earlier for a glass of wine. (That was his nickname throughout North London in the 1960s and 1970s, so I can hardly call him anything else.)

Peter had introduced some of the boys to wine and cocktails as a change from beer or lager. We grew up with Peter and never cared about his sexuality. He was one of the firm, and had our full protection and respect; if another firm insulted him, they paid a hefty price, usually at the hands of Eddie. Those massive hands were not to be messed with. Once, when someone from another firm said Peter was 'a lovely boy', the result was a broken jaw and a harsh warning for all to see.

'You told me twice that there was bad news and I heard you the first time, darling,' Peter pranced around and told Tony off, as usual. 'I'm not deaf, you know. You only need to say things once.'

Peter talked a little bit posh. We all talked like Cockneys, but he used some fancy words. He had an air of authority about him. If he walked into a room, immaculately dressed, with his blond hair perfectly combed, you would think he was a male model, or maybe a banker or something like that. He was no mug; he was well educated, and his old man worked in the City.

Peter was always around when we were growing up. We'd always thought he was a little bit unusual. While the boys played football, he would be skipping with the girls. As he got older, he became an out-and-out crook. He was like us, but was more into fraud with cards and cheques. He would do shoplifting and that sort of thing – soft stuff, as we called it.

Our gay friend had a terrific eye for fashion. And he really knew all about it. If I went shopping with him, I would put some gear on and ask, 'How do I look, Peter?' He would say, 'No … mmm, that shirt doesn't go with that tie, darling.'

The women all fancied him, but he would tell them, 'Oh, sweetheart, I'm no good for you – but I could be good for your brother.' He was unavailable, and that made them want him even more.

And his pad was like a showroom. The rest of us had little two-bedroom flats, but his place was fitted out with modern, arty gear. He did a lot of shopping, but he didn't pay for anything in his pad – it was all stolen!

I remember one day he came round to our house, looking like a male model as usual, and wearing make-up.

My dad said, 'What are you doing with all that make-up on, Peter?'

'I'm gay, Mr Cummines,' Peter replied.

My mum, cooking in the kitchen, heard what was being said and poked her head into the lounge. 'Oh, that's good, we're all happy in this house.'

'He doesn't mean that,' my dad said with a laugh. 'He's a pansy.'

'Don't say that,' my mum said, looking a little concerned. 'He'll get better. You'll get better, won't you, Peter?'

I can't blame Mum for her reaction; in the 1960s and 1970s people didn't tend to 'come out' like Peter.

Back in the Enkel Arms, waiting for me to make my mind up on what to do about Stavros and Eva's daughter, Peter and Tony were having a squabble about who was the better thief. Peter said that Tony was a 'jump-up merchant', which meant that he jumped up and stole things from the backs of lorries. Peter said his own stuff came from Harrods or Fortnum and Mason, while Tony's gear came from Woolworths. After their short diversion, they looked at me to see if a decision had been reached about getting involved in the chip shop crisis.

We did have a democratic process, discussing the work to be done. If anyone didn't want to get involved, they had the chance to duck out. I listened to everyone's views, took everything into account and made my decision. I always had the final say.

In those days, if people had a problem, they didn't go to the Old Bill; they didn't want to be known as police informants or grasses. Instead, they would go to the head of the local manor – in this case, that was me. All the way through, from the early street gangs to the heavy firms, I evolved as the natural leader. That never changed. Also, people close to me knew that if they did not do as they were told, they would be shot. I was prepared to carry out the threat, whereas others might have shirked that brutal solution.

'Let's do it,' I said, finishing the last mouthful of bitter lemon.

I left Tony to his twitching and drinking and decided to pay his Greek Cypriot friends a visit, just around the corner. When I arrived at the shop, I could see they were genuine, hard-working people; they had their aprons on and were grafting away in the chip shop. The girl's dad, Stavros, was small and podgy; he had a receding hairline but greasy strands remained and straddled his face. The fat was sizzling, excited voices relayed the food orders and, at first sight, everything looked normal.

Stavros took me upstairs, where his wife, Eva, was in tears. She was also a short lady, and looked totally worn out with all the worry. She had dark rings under her eyes and the problems of her troubled family were obviously weighing heavily on her shoulders.

'We just want these people to go away,' they both sobbed. 'We'll give you anything. Just say what you want. Our daughter is in danger here.' Stavros produced a biscuit tin full of rolled-up notes. It was the family life savings, really.

I wondered why they preferred a biscuit tin to the bank next door, but that was their business.

'You can have it all,' Stavros said. 'We just need this problem to go away. We're terrified of these people and what they're doing to our daughter.'

'I don't want any money,' I answered, angry at the way the family was being treated. 'I'll make the problem go away.'

'You must take some money,' he pleaded, handing me the tin and prodding bunches of notes.

'Look, Stavros, I don't want your savings. If any of my family comes into your shop, they get free fish and chips for life. Is that OK? If my mum comes round, she gets a free supper. That will be your payment.'

Stavros's face lit up. 'Do you really mean that?'

I really meant it. He gave me the names I needed, and the address: the Turkish brothers had a little lock-up garage where they repaired cars.

I walked back over to the pub and nodded to Old Frank. He was up to speed with all my ideas, even though he was twenty years older and from another generation. I always admired him for having such a young outlook.

'Go and get Kennedy,' I ordered.

'Going on a bit of work, are we?'

'Yeah, yeah. Go and get Kennedy. I need to see that he's ready for action. Let's do it.'

Old Frank assumed we would be off on another armed robbery. He went to get the gun from its hiding place and reappeared in his car. It was an unremarkable-looking 1970s Vauxhall Cavalier 1.6GL, in a disgusting brown colour, with velour trim. Yes, it was a horrible-looking vehicle, and that was the idea. It was totally anonymous; there was no point in screeching around in a flashy Jag during an armed robbery.

We kept everything as low profile as possible to keep the coppers at bay – and the Cavalier didn't really have a 1.6 engine. My mechanic Brucie had installed a souped-up lump in there – probably twice the size of the original. It rocketed from 0 to 60 in about nine seconds and kept going like shit off a shovel. Top speed? I've no idea. It was all a bit of a blur, and the average cop car stood no chance of keeping up. Brucie had also fitted suspension and brakes to cope with the mean machine's awesome power.

I'll never forget Frank braking from 100 miles an hour to a standstill if anything blocked our path. The normal practice was to brace yourself as if for a crash landing, and hang on because your life depended on it – no one wore seatbelts in those days, of course. Religious types usually muttered a prayer or two.

Outside the Enkel Arms, Frank emerged from that wolf-in-sheep's-clothing and slipped me Kennedy for the once-over. I scrutinised the gun to make sure everything was in perfect condition.

'OK, Kennedy is good to go. Pick me up at seven o'clock in the morning. It's an early job for "the stinger".'

The next morning, Frank arrived at my house in his suit exactly on time. I was also immaculately dressed, as usual.

All suited and booted for the 'stinger' raid, then, I checked the gun over again. I scrutinised the two hammers and two triggers, and made sure Kennedy was in prime condition to fire. I inserted one cartridge which contained the normal buckshot. I filled the other cartridge with hard rock salt.

The idea was that you could shoot someone and damage their legs, but the salt melted into their wounds, so the name 'stinger' was ideal. Despite intense pain, the wounds would heal, leaving no trace for any forensics people. The weapon was used in the underworld as a punishment tool.

I have to tell you that there was violence going on all over London in the 1970s. Inter-gang warfare was commonplace; people were getting cut, and shot in drive-by shootings. When they were hurt, they didn't go to the doctor or hospital, because that would attract the attention of the Old Bill.

It was also common for the inter-gang rivalry to spill over to outside London. If a member of a firm had overstepped the mark, he could be set up at a bogus meeting in the country somewhere like Kent, Surrey or Sussex, to avoid attention. He would then be attacked with baseball bats or shot in the legs.

We pulled up outside the garage. The doors were open. One of the brothers was working under a car so Old Frank and I walked straight through the door and aimed at his legs. The gun went off, blasting him with the salt. He writhed in agony and I left him to scream. He probably thought he had been peppered with real pellets. He screamed and he screamed. The sound of someone making that noise, thinking that death is the next step, has to be heard to be believed. I knew that sound off by heart.

'We ain't done nothing wrong,' he bleated as he screamed. 'What do you want with us?'

They knew why I was there. A few seconds later Old Frank and I walked into their little office and placed Kennedy carefully against the older brother's head. The live round was left in the shotgun, and I am sure he knew his days could be numbered. He stared at the hammer, as it hovered over the cartridge. His eyes began to bulge and he shook with fear. I could smell and taste that fear.

I can't say I got any enjoyment from what I was doing: it was just a bit of work. I was doing a job, like a plumber fixing a washing machine. It's true that I felt a rush of power in the early days when I held my first pistol, that sort of thing, but the business side took over after that, until I was just simply doing my job.

'If you ain't off the manor in twenty-four hours, I am going to blow the pair of your fucking heads off. So it's best that you're gone. Just this one warning. Your brother there has been shot with rock salt. He'll recover. This one is a couple of inches from your brain, and it's a live round. Do you want your workshop redecorated?'

They were gone in twenty-four hours. Problem solved. Everyone in the manor knew the 'Turkish Terrors' had been removed; no one liked those scumbags dealing in drugs and getting young girls to work in the streets.

People sometimes say we should have just upended the pair at the garage, with a few well-aimed punches but, on this occasion, I knew the fist would have been only a temporary measure.

I heard that they went back to wherever they came from in the first place. Other people got to hear about the 'stinger' incident. If the brothers had gone on another manor, people would have been on to them straight away, keeping a constant watch. They would never have been able to operate.

Sorted.

Later that day I headed off for a drink in the local nightclub, the Log Cabin in Caledonian Road. It was time to catch up with the boys and get updates on our protection rackets and armed robberies.

'Have a drink, Bobby,' they all said at once, as I entered.

'Go on then, I'll have a bitter lemon.'

The firm were all there, enjoying a drink and a catch-up. I felt like a Robin Hood character, having restored law and order, although my methods were definitely outside the law. The 'stinger' was well outside the law.

'Nice one, nice one,' Tony the Greek said, buying me another drink and refilling everyone's glass. 'Thank you. Thank you.'

Tony, dressed in his latest John Travolta-type gear, complete with flares, was twitching less than normal and seemed to be thrilled with the outcome. The job had been much heavier than his everyday work, so he had no intention of discussing the finer points of the operation.

'Well sorted. Best thing that could happen to them pieces of shit. Total lowlife,' Eddie the mountainous minder pointed out, keeping the conversation away from our tactics. Eddie always said that you never knew who was listening. He clenched and unclenched his fists, showing a hand made up of fingers the size of jumbo sausages.

'It wasn't personal, Eddie. I didn't know these people. It was all business. We're not gangsters, fucking up people's lives for no reason. We don't take liberties with working-class people. They were just thugs, advertising the fact that they were gangsters.'

Alan, another wheel man, was a bit of a comedian. He'd heard about the payment for sorting out the Greek/Turkish problem, announcing to everyone that the Turkish issue had been resolved, with no more action needed. He then announced that I had refused cash for the job, and made a general observation to his attentive audience: 'If Bobby did that for a bag of chips, what would he do for a pickled onion?'

The 'stinger' incident shows that, in those days, firms ruled their manors and people didn't want to go to the police. Anyone who reported a crime to coppers found themselves in a difficult position: they had to give evidence in court and all that sort of thing – they didn't want the aggravation. They knew they would come up against a smart-arsed brief whose job was to save the guy he represented. People just didn't want all that. The last thing they needed was police around their house, taking statements. All they wanted to do was to get on with their lives.

When the victims went into court they became the victims. So they thought, *'I've seen it happen to other people and I don't want that. I can talk to someone and we can sort it out that way.'*

And that was how it worked with our own system of dispensing justice. Instead of getting a slap on the wrist in court and told off for being a naughty boy, the villain received a slap on the jaw. No matter what your intellectual capacity was, no matter what language you spoke: if I hit you on the chin, you knew I had the hump with you.

The police went on nicking people. Often, they realised they didn't have the right person to fit the crime, but they knew when a guy was 'bang at it'. They knew he was a crook, causing them time and aggravation, and they wanted to put him away.

So they went to court and told lies to get him out of the way. It was a sort of moral dilemma – a pious perjury, if you like. They knew what he was up to, but they couldn't prove it. That practice still goes on today.

I remember coppers coming round to the manor to chat to us. They knew someone had done something really terrible, but they couldn't get him for it, so they sat in the pub with our firm.

They were very cunning. They would tell us about the toe-rag and how they couldn't nick him because there wasn't enough evidence. The message was that if the guy could be sorted out, the coppers wouldn't come back to investigate: if we wanted someone ejected from the manor, the coppers were prepared to turn a blind eye. The scheme worked a treat.

There were so many rumours about what I'd done and hadn't done it was getting ridiculous. I even heard that I'd dumped a body in Hampstead Ponds wrapped up in a carpet. That was just a wind-up; the Old Bill investigated a load of stuff that didn't really happen. Some of it did, of course, but they were having a hard time separating fact from fiction.

Another legendary tale involves a knife, a lunchbox, a wardrobe and a flask of tea.

A guy was going around taking money off people and bullying them. He took money off a young kid, about thirteen, who had a few bob. He was quite a big kid and he tried to have a fight with the bully. The older geezer was around eighteen or twenty. He just pulled out a blade from his pocket and cut the kid on the arm with it.

The kid's dad was really angry because this guy was violent. This was a nasty bully. He was taking money out of people's wages on the building sites when they got paid on Thursdays, and that sort of trash. The guy was even taking money off his own mother. He terrorised her a bit and then she got him moved out, so he lived in a flat on his own. I heard people saying he always carried a weapon and threatened people. I thought he might be on drugs, the way he was carrying on.

The dad said to me: 'Bobby, he's doing it to elderly people and geezers coming home from work, taking twenty quid out of their wage packets. He's a total menace and now he's cut my boy. Something has to be done, Bobby.' The dad was offering a hundred quid to sort the guy out.

The only way to sort him out, really, was to do him some damage.

One Thursday, after the guy had threatened people at the building sites and taken money off them, he went into his flat, had a shower and went into his bedroom to change. He opened up his wardrobe door and someone came out and cut him.

The rumour went about that it was me. People were saying that I sat in the wardrobe and waited for him. They said the attacker, whoever it was, sat in his wardrobe with a packed lunch, waiting for the bully. As time went on, people even said the guy had a picnic basket in there with him.

Who attacked the bully? Nothing was ever proved. Someone cut him anyway, and cut him up pretty badly, but he left the manor and didn't come back again, so the problem was solved.

Rough justice, maybe, but the garage brothers had to be stopped and the same applied to the pay-day bully. There was no other way.

CHAPTER FIVE

FIRMS AT WAR

Old Frank the driver always had his ear to the ground. He had dozens of contacts who fed him pieces of information. Old Frank put them all together like a jigsaw and worked out exactly what was happening on and off the manor.

Our money-making schemes were bringing in several grand a week. He knew people were after some of our business, and that a great deal of aggro was on the cards.

'I reckon there's going to be a ruck tonight,' Old Frank warned me, during an unexpected Sunday morning phone call. 'A couple of firms are getting greedy. I heard they've been sniffing around the manor.'

I made some more enquiries. A girl we knew told us that a firm in Upper Street, Islington, had talked about cutting me up and throwing me to the dogs. I'd heard such bollocks before and normally took no notice. But when she said they were tooling up for a ruck, well, that was different.

I knew the aggressive firm and sent them a message to meet us at Highbury Fields, where we would put them in their place.

A scribbled note came back, addressed to me: 'We're looking forward to it!'

I sent a car round to Islington with another note, outlining the terms of engagement. I suggested ten men a side. There were to be no rules, apart from a ban on guns. Frank loaded Kennedy in the motor just in case they pulled one on us.

I arranged to meet my firm in the Enkel Arms. All were tooled up to the hilt. Neil, one of the best fighters, had a razor at the ready. I'd picked up a wartime bayonet for a couple of quid; it was so sharp you couldn't touch the edge. It had a metal sheath to hide the blade and prevent any accidents. Old Frank was a small man, and he was almost dwarfed by his fearsome-looking iron bar; Chrissy and Andy the Greek had sharpened their evil-looking knives for the occasion.

We crouched over a table in the corner of the bar, like a rugby team in a huddle, and vowed to fight like tigers. Then we crammed into three motors with our accessories and headed for the Fields, each of us determined to rip the rival firm to shreds. I know it sounds grim, but that's what it was like; we had to protect our interests and avoid being booted off the patch by a bunch of scumbags.

Davey, our reconnaissance man, went ahead on a spying mission. We had to make sure that we weren't heading into a trap. I feared an ambush close to the location, but that didn't happen. We parked up about half a mile away and Davey did his stuff; he came back and reported that the

Islington mob was there, hanging around the Fields and waiting for us, as arranged.

Even in that dark, cold air, you could feel violence in the atmosphere; you could detect an animal-like ferocity; you could sense that death or serious injury was more than likely. And I was the main target. I knew that, because I was the leader and they would try to take me out first. Also I'd slagged off the opposition on a previous occasion because I hated the way they went about their business. They showed no loyalty to anyone.

The gangs faced up to each other and Chrissy ran straight into the mob with his blade flashing. He was thrusting in all directions and took one guy by complete surprise. Chrissy tried to slash his face, but the bloke put up his hand and his palm was badly cut instead. A stream of blood shot out of his arm, and Chrissy kept flashing his blade around, cutting and cutting. Someone grabbed Chrissy's victim, covered him in towels to soak up the blood and then carted him off. That guy must have been close to death.

As I weighed in with my bayonet, I could see a group had gone after Chrissy: two or three went at him hard with iron bars and beat him as he lay on the ground. I moved in with the bayonet and kept them off him, but at the same time I was battered with a lump of wood. I could feel blood running down my face; my back felt like it was breaking up.

This was getting serious. I caused as much damage as I could; all around me, men were crying like babies as they tried to stem the flow of blood from their injuries. In the middle of North London a horrendous battle was happening, fought by a bunch of savages. I struggled to breathe after a vicious blow from an iron bar.

As twenty or so yelling men hacked away at each other in medieval style, sirens pierced the night air. It was the Old Bill; by the sound of things, they were arriving in force. Both sides in the fray halted combat and, almost as one, limped and crawled to the getaway cars and made rapid arrangements for treatment. Hospital was out of the question with the Old Bill swarming all over the place.

Chrissy was in a bad way. 'What day is it? What happened? What the fuck is going on?'

'Everything's sweet,' I lied. 'We've had an accident, but we're on our way for help, so don't worry.'

Chrissy had been so badly beaten around the head that he was concussed, making no sense and continuing to bleed. Our two getaway cars with enormous, souped-up engines raced away from our pursuers. Our destination: the Major's house.

The Major was an absolute diamond who'd served as a medic in the army during the war. We knew he wouldn't call any police or hospitals or anything like that. He was used to patching up wounds in the heat of battle. He had a regiment's supply of field dressings – and we needed rolls and rolls of the stuff. Chrissy looked like an Egyptian mummy when the Major had finished with him, and I was also well wrapped up. Old Frank was badly cut from razor wounds. Davey, Andy the Greek and three younger helpers from the manor had minor cuts and bruises, which the Major sorted out in a matter of minutes.

I lay on the Major's couch as he checked out my ribs; I could tell a few were broken, and the Major pointed to the problem areas, caused by a ferocious swing of a rusty old iron bar. The Major actually looked like an army officer, if you know what I mean. He was tall, with thin lips and a neatly trimmed moustache. He must have been around forty-five to fifty years old with short, receding hair. He also had a crimson face and large reddish ears. I assumed it was all to do with his blood pressure, and we weren't helping to bring that down.

I told our battered gang to hang around for a few hours while we recovered some more. A roll call in the morning established that most of our walking wounded would head for Andy's house. We didn't need the Major to tell us that Chrissy was in no fit state to go anywhere. He was barely conscious, and had several swellings as big as footballs.

'Is it a hospital job?' I asked, hoping that the Major would rule out that option. 'They'll call the Old Bill, but we might have no choice.'

'Give him a couple of days,' the Major tried to reassure me. 'Some of that swelling has to go down. I'm worried about his head injuries. If there's no improvement, I'll take him to casualty. They won't believe he's been in a car crash, so I'll have to come clean.'

'Understood,' I nodded as we clambered aboard our two motors, looking like a sorry bunch of war victims.

Back at Andy's house, we laughed and boasted about our exploits. We exaggerated our fighting skills, of course, and we all had tales of amazing bravado during the duel.

When our wounds healed, we went in search of the other firm. We found them in a café and handed out such a hiding. The café owner had never seen anything like it; we almost knocked their heads off. They gave us no more trouble after that.

There were so many stories spreading about me that I had to do something. My girlfriend at the time said a violent guy on the manor, called Johnny, was telling people that I'd been shooting and cutting rivals throughout North London. Well, some of it was true but a lot of it was bollocks. This bloke also told the girl she was going out with I was a gangster; I told her the word should be 'businessman', as I wasn't a mindless thug.

Down to business, then. She pointed out my victim in a pub – I knew who he was – and I called Old Frank to the scene. He was always my first point of call with his mean machine and reliability. Old Frank, of course, also had access to my store of weapons. They were locked away in a secret place, which I still can't divulge.

'Could you bring Kennedy's brother?' I urged from a phone box near the Hercules pub in Holloway Road. It was an older-style building on a street corner, not far from Arsenal tube station.

Within minutes I heard Frank's throaty exhaust pulsating along the street and I could see his small frame, sitting bolt upright in the driver's seat. He drew up in a dark lane near the pub. I made a quick check of the area, slid into the driver's seat of that ordinary-looking Vauxhall and accepted a cigarette from my mate.

'Do you have Kennedy's brother?'

'Under the seat,' Frank confirmed.

'Loaded?'

'Loaded.'

'Let's go,' I hissed.

Kennedy's brother was a Smith & Wesson .38 revolver. It fitted neatly under my jacket.

I spotted Johnny at the bar, gorging on a gigantic steak, being as loud as ever and shooting his mouth off; he was a real fucking one-man crowd. He stood there, shouting in his shiny leather jacket, chunky gold rings and bracelets, an arrogant snarl all over his face.

'Oi, it's Bobby and Old Frank!' he boomed. 'Couple of drinks over there for those boys.'

'Johnny, I need a word with you. Something's come up. Best not to talk in here. Let's go outside.'

I left Old Frank with our drinks – a pint and my usual bitter lemon – and shepherded Johnny to an alleyway at the side of the pub. Johnny thought, as he was a good creeper – burglar – that I had some work for him.

I pushed Johnny up against the wall and his whole body – including his overhanging beer belly – quivered as I stuck the barrel of the revolver into his big mouth. I chose my words carefully.

'I'll tell you this once. If I ever hear that you've been talking about me again, especially calling me a gangster, you can look forward to your next meal. It will be fed up a plastic tube, and that's if you make it to intensive care.'

He pleaded for his life. 'Christ, what's going on? Don't shoot me ... don't shoot me.'

'I am not a gangster,' I spat. 'I'm a businessman trying hard to earn a crust. Understood?'

I didn't give him time to reply. I took the barrel out of his mouth and smashed him in the face with the butt. His lip split, but he wasn't a dead man, and he seemed to appreciate that his life had been spared.

He spluttered his thanks: 'OK, you're not a gangster. You are not a gangster.'

I pushed him back into the pub, nodded to Frank and we prepared to leave. I told the barman to pour our drinks down the drain, which he did without making any comment. Frank and I breezed off into the night. Job done, and Johnny kept his huge, ignorant mouth shut.

The jealousy about the schemes in our manor didn't stop, though. I was forever watching my back because my contacts kept warning me about other firms with ambitions.

A few weeks later I was walking through Holloway, minding my own business. I was on my way to check on my business interests, and have a drink with some of our firm. Perhaps that day I'd taken my eye off the ball; perhaps I should have been on the lookout for any trouble.

Crack! A gun fired and I felt that my leg had been set on

fire. The pain was unbearable. Through the pain I could hear, 'Bobby's been shot! Bobby's been shot!'

I knew it was a drive-by because, after the bullet hit, I saw a cloud of exhaust smoke and heard a motor revving. Apart from that, it was all about pain and the lads yelling out instructions about how to treat the wound. Chrissy, amazingly enough, had been out drinking with us after his partial recovery. He still walked with a limp and boasted a few scars. He wrapped his coat around my leg.

As usual, I ended up back at the Major's pad. He poured antiseptic on the wound, and I have to say that if Kennedy's brother had been nearby it would have been used on the Major. The pain was the worst I have ever felt in my life.

The Major knew his guns. 'It was a .22 rifle. Look, the bullet has gone straight through your leg. But it's only a flesh wound. A little more to the left and you would have lost your knee cap.'

'Thanks, Major,' was all I could manage, relieved to still be attached to my knee.

He was an expert with plastic skin, so he sprayed on the substance, which helps with the healing process. By this time my knee was twice its normal size; I gulped down the Major's painkillers in a desperate move to feel better. They did help, and probably took about half the pain away. I paid the Major his £50 fee and ended up at the house of Chrissy's mother. She looked after me and changed the bandages for several weeks.

Revenge. It is such a short word, but has so much meaning. The boys were determined to get full revenge on my attacker. As it happened, they didn't wait for me to recover; they took matters into their own hands.

As I lay on the couch at Chrissy's mum's place with my leg in the air a few days later, I was happy to learn that my attacker would have to sleep on his belly for the foreseeable future. The guy was a minor enforcer called Joe – his job with his firm was to intimidate people who were being ripped off and make sure that they paid their fees for protection and a host of other rackets. It was a bad move to try to put me on the sidelines.

The boys had found out he was responsible, went to find him, bent him over a wall and cut his arse. He was in agony every time he went for a poo, and I took some satisfaction from that.

I had no regrets from any of my actions. Anyone who suffered at my hands from a premeditated act deserved it: the end game, for me, was always money.

The boys had found out that the .22 rifle belonged to Joe's dad. I decided to pass the time by writing a brief note to the father:

'I suggest that your boy sticks to darts. He wouldn't have won a teddy at the fairground with that shooting. I know he'll be in more pain than me at the moment.'

Well, a note came back in an envelope. The note offered an apology and the package bulged with £500. No further action needed.

I was making too many enemies. Shortly after the rifle incident, a shotgun was fired from another passing car. The pellets hit Big Eddie, who wasn't badly hurt, but he vowed revenge on the spot. He took note of the car number, went off to have his wounds treated by the Major, and appeared at my house the next morning with a beaming grin.

'Eh? You've just been peppered with pellets and you're grinning.'

'I've had a result,' Eddie announced. 'I've found out who fired the pellets, and he is definitely no friend of yours. Do you remember a bloke from the ruck, with earrings and long, greasy black hair?'

'How could I forget? He whacked me on the back with that iron bar and I can still feel it.'

'I've just been to see him. I borrowed Kennedy's brother from Old Frank. Hope you don't mind.'

'No, no, that's OK,' I answered, growing more curious by the second. 'What the fuck happened?'

'Well, I ...'

'Go on,' I ordered. 'What the fuck did you do?'

Big Eddie produced the revolver, cradled it in his huge hands, and laid it on the dining-room table.

'Kennedy's brother can be well pleased with his work tonight. He was fired through the letterbox but seems to have hit a sensitive area. Your greasy friend isn't the man he was.'

I had the last word: 'I hope you're not talking bollocks!'

After that, the banter turned into a nightmare because a bit of work went wrong. It went badly wrong. Someone died.

We'd heard about a large amount of wages being stored in a house – around £30,000 or £40,000. We had to tie up the people – that's called a wrap-up – while we looked for the cash. We found a lot of it, but a gun went off accidentally.

I had tied up one of the people and one of the gags was too tight. The noise of the gun caused panic and one of the group choked on their own vomit. We had to run off because of the noise from the gun, and couldn't check on the gags. That was a disaster for all the families involved.

I was staying at my parents' house when the murder squad arrived. I was having a cup of tea with Mum and Dad when there was a knock at the door.

A couple of coppers came in and my mum asked, 'What's going on? Who do you want?'

'We've come for Robert,' one of them answered, as my mum started to cry.

'What do you want him for?' my dad asked, hoping that one of my insurance rackets had been rumbled.

'We're going to charge him with murder.'

The room fell silent. Mum looked at me and just sobbed and sobbed. Dad stared at me and shook his head. I had failed them both. And I was still just nineteen years old.

I stood trial for murder and was found not guilty. I was found guilty of manslaughter because the jury could see that it was an accident.

While I have no remorse for anything I've done in my life, over the years that unnecessary death has haunted me.

I was sentenced to seven and a half years, which was fair enough under the circumstances. I served five years, firstly at Aylesbury Young Offenders Institution and then, when I was twenty-one, they moved me to Maidstone.

Aylesbury was a violent place where prisoners were treated like dogs, and I couldn't wait to get away from there. I was singled out as the most violent person in Aylesbury and they gave me some unbelievable treatment.

One time I was called down to the medical room. I assumed it was for a check-up or something like that.

'We want you to take these,' a doctor said, holding out some pills. 'Don't worry, they won't harm you.'

Well, I didn't have much choice and so I swallowed this cocktail of drugs, wondering what was coming next.

After I'd taken the drugs I was whisked off to another prison – not sure where – in a dazed state.

When I arrived there, a screw said: 'Don't take the cuffs off. This one is really violent.'

They took me to a room where everything was white – it looked like something from a private hospital. I was given another load of tablets; I believe now that they didn't know that I'd had the previous lot. The double dose meant that I was absolutely stoned out of my nut.

They sat me on a chair, took my shirt off, and left me with just my trousers on. Next, a guy – who looked like a doctor – produced a set of electrodes with suckers on the end. They attached them to my head and body and injected the suckers with some sort of jelly.

The next thing I knew, a strobe light was flashing in my face. Bang! Bang! Bang! The light flashed, flashed and flashed.

Then someone said, 'OK.'

They switched some sort of current on and I felt it pulse through my body. My muscles tensed up. The current seemed to go off and on, jolting me five or six times. The room was going round and round and I was sweating like a pig. I could see rivers of sweat pouring down my body.

Through the haze I could see blurred figures monitoring me. A long list of thoughts flooded my head: *'What sort of experiment is this? Why are they doing it? This has to be illegal! Who's keeping records? Am I at the hands of the Gestapo? What drugs have they given me? Am I going to die?'*

I must have passed out, because the next thing I knew I was back in my original prison cell at Aylesbury. It was night time and a prison officer, Mr Ward, was sitting next to my bed.

'What the fuck happened?' I asked, still more than a bit woozy.

'You'll be all right, son,' he said, looking concerned.

Mr Ward was a decent man, and I could tell he was unhappy at my treatment. He was upset and his face said it all. He wouldn't go into any details and walked off.

I had a thumping headache. I know people have migraines, but this was a migraine on a massive scale. My head ached and ached for a couple of weeks.

My sister Pauline came to see me and demanded to know why I had peculiar red marks on my head. No one would tell her. It was all hushed up. I was sent off to other prisons, my wounds healed, and I am still brimming with anger to this day.

All those clandestine activities were hushed up. Nothing was logged; any relevant paperwork disappeared. Prisoners who had the treatment were ghosted off to other prisons, making it difficult for relatives to trace them. By the time visits were arranged the bruises – caused by those little copper suckers on the prisoner's head – had vanished.

There was no national outcry. Stories abounded about these barbaric treatments, but what could be proved?

The 'liquid cosh' method of strong tranquillisers took over: fit men were taken away, only to return as zombies. They even used the stuff on Reggie Kray. Soon, he was so used to those drugs that he drank them by the cupful.

When they moved me to Maidstone, I saw that many prisoners were on LSD, but I still encountered some clever criminals. I couldn't wait to get out and continue my career in the armed robbery business.

But how long would I last before being nicked for good?

CHAPTER SIX
GANGSTERS, BUSINESSMEN AND POLITICIANS

I always hated being referred to as a gangster. I never wanted to be a gangster nor saw myself as one – as you saw with the story about Johnny the big mouth. I was a businessman, involved in the business of crime.

In my day there were three types of criminal, jostling for position. As well as the universally hated gangsters, and business people like me, you had the opportunist.

In the modern age, things are much the same. The opportunists get involved out of necessity. They may be on low incomes or have to support a drug habit. They have no other means of earning money, like a steady job. They usually have poor education and problems in their background. They are also victims of crime themselves and get caught in a vicious circle. When I hear politicians talking about taking away their benefits, I think this is insanity. Without benefits, these people will be driven into the hands of drug dealers and organised criminals. They will be even more desperate to get money to support themselves and their families, and so fuel the crime industry.

We encountered gangsters in the pubs and night clubs, dressing loudly, talking even louder and using violence to show they were tough. They were loud, abrasive and generally a pain in the arse. These people were known to us all as the one-man crowd. They became more of a liability in the crime business than an asset, because they brought criminal activities to the attention of the public, police and media. That was a nightmare for the real movers and shakers within the business, who were motivated purely by money and had no intention of carrying out violence just for the sake of it.

The gangsters wanted everyone to know that they operated outside the law to glamorise their own existence. It was as if the gangster had a badge stamped on his forehead saying, 'Please nick me so that I can prove I am a gangster.' The police were always happy to oblige.

The reason I didn't like being around thugs and gangsters was because they were unpredictable, and prone to outbreaks of senseless violence at the drop of a hat. Those around them could never feel safe, could never relax or enjoy an evening out.

Because of my previous lifestyle and built-in animal instincts of survival, even to this day I can walk into a pub, club or any place, and pick out the guy carrying a weapon. I can detect tension in the air and I have a good idea if things are going to kick off. That is why I try to avoid those types of places. Booze and gangsters are a recipe for total disaster. Those thugs should stick to bitter lemon.

I remember one evening when I was out with some of the boys for a quiet meeting. It was with an Irish guy called Pat, who'd invited us over to his manor for a drink and to discuss a bit of work. He was a friend of Tony the Greek and worked in a warehouse. The owner of the warehouse was going bankrupt and wanted to sell off the majority of his stock before the official receivers came in to impound it.

We arrived in the pub in north-west London. It was a big Victorian building with tired décor inside. It was an Irish place, where a band played jigs and the local community jumped around to the traditional music. The band was the real deal, but I reckoned Pat should have chosen a better venue – there was something off about the place.

The air was full of smoke, the smell of stale beer and cheap perfume, aftershave and all that. I didn't feel at home. We stood out like sore thumbs in our three-piece suits. The sight of me, standing there all suited and booted and drinking bitter lemon, must have seemed strange to the locals, but, as ever, I was determined to keep a clear head at all times.

Pat was a really nice, run-of-the mill guy and I was very impressed with his cheerful attitude and good manners. Good manners have always been a big winner for me; I hate bad-mannered people.

Tony the Greek got the drinks in as usual, and Pat explained the deal to us. He showed me the list of stock they wanted to unload and the price list it sold for, plus the price they wanted from us. After a bit of haggling on the price, we agreed to meet up with him to discuss payment terms, delivery and all that.

Once that was done we shook hands and then talked in general about other stuff Pat was involved in. Although he was an ordinary bloke, Pat was a bit of a ducker and diver like Tony the Greek and always had things to sell. I liked him and respected him. I felt that we could do a lot of business in the future. Tony had already assured me of Pat's reliability and that he was a 'closed-mouth guy'. I felt safe doing business with him.

As I bought our second round of drinks I noticed that there were two blokes and a woman involved in an argument. All had had too much to drink and their voices became louder and more aggressive. It was none of our business, so we carried on with our chat and let them get on with it.

Then, suddenly, all hell broke loose. Two blokes threw right-handers at each other, bottles and glasses started flying and others started joining in. It really kicked off. A bottle just missed the head of my brother, Frankie, and Tony copped a punch in the side of the head. I chinned the guy who did that and more fists flew.

I felt a punch in the stomach and carried on throwing right-handers at those near us. We heard the sound of police cars arriving, which meant it was time for us to leave. As we stumbled out of the pub and headed for our car, I felt a burning sensation in my gut. I felt a wet patch and assumed it was from the contents of the glasses flying around. As we drove along I had a closer look. There was blood everywhere; it was *my* fucking blood. One of those bastards in the pub had stabbed me, and it was quite a cut.

I grabbed Tony's scarf and held it against the wound to stem the flow. It was a nasty wound and I knew we were looking at a hospital job, but I knew they would tell the police about a knife wound, so I had to get my story straight.

The bogus tale went along the lines that I had been boning a piece of meat for a party, but the knife had slipped and I'd accidentally stabbed myself. The doctor in the A&E raised an eyebrow at that explanation and pointed out that it was a nasty wound, very near to a main artery. He said I could easily have bled to death.

The law came and I stuck to my story, so they pissed off. They were probably pleased that I had been stabbed and they had no work to do with their investigations. I received twenty-six stitches for my night out, and a ruined suit. I should have headed off to another pub when I felt the tension in the first place. I still have the scar today, as a brutal reminder of how mindless violence can affect people for the rest of their lives.

Still, we completed the deal with Pat and he was full of apologies, although it wasn't his fault. It wasn't our fault, either. It was a case of being in the wrong place at the wrong time. When two gangsters start a brawl over an old pub trollop, it's time to make yourself scarce.

The incident made me even more aware how you can be an innocent bystander and still end up as a victim of violent crime. It can happen to anyone. The worst thing was that, because we were out on a social bit of business, none of us had been tooled up. That reminded me of the old rule: better to be caught with a tool when you don't need it, than be caught without one when you do need it.

On the other hand, if you do violence to others, you can't complain when it happens to you. What goes around comes around.

But there is another twist to this story because, weeks after I had the stitches taken out, I was having lunch with the guys in our favourite Greek restaurant.

Andy the Greek brought up the incident in the pub and I said, 'It's fucking outrageous that you can't go out for a quiet drink and do a bit of business without some lunatic fucking stabbing you. What is this world coming to? The problem is that too many people are getting hold of blades these days.'

Everyone agreed, and then Old Frank the driver started laughing.

'What's going on?' I demanded to know.

'Well, I was just thinking about you – tools and blades and everything. It's all a bit rich, coming from you!'

I agreed he had a point, but reminded him that I was trying to do business and not cause mayhem in a pub for no reason.

The Kray and Richardson gangs are perfect examples of how gangsters differ from criminal businessmen. Reggie, Ronnie and his thugs had the brawn, while Charlie, Eddie and the rest of the Richardson outfit had the brains. The

Krays wanted the image and notoriety of being seen as hardened gangsters – the same as those portrayed in Humphrey Bogart and James Cagney movies. They had no idea about business or setting up profitable scams. They dealt in violence, thuggery and glamour.

The Richardson gang, on the other hand, was far more sophisticated in its practices, running complex frauds known as 'long firms'. This involved building up trust with a supplier over a long period of time and always paying on the dot. Once the supplier's confidence was sky high, a large order was placed. No cheque was handed over this time; the goods and the Richardsons disappeared, and market stalls were flooded with the latest kettles, irons and an impressive range of household goods.

The Richardsons were also involved in mineral deals in South Africa and Canada. They were far ahead of their time in the crime business. They were businessmen motivated by the desire for wealth. Charlie Richardson's knowledge of minerals was second to none, and he had an astonishing brain for business. If he'd been born on the right side of the tracks, he would have run a multinational company, he was that good. To this day I have not come across his equal.

When I was active, the criminal businessmen were the real deal. This group wanted to get money with the least attention to themselves and their activities. That was my involvement in crime, from start to finish.

Businessmen in the crime business of the 1970s normally ran well-structured outfits, had good organisational skills and kept their activities out of sight. As far as the rest of the world was concerned, nothing dodgy could be detected. It was all about the money and not the glamorous image. On the other hand, these people were totally ruthless; if need be, they killed to remove any obstacles standing in the way of their business.

Contract killing was used by criminal businessmen as a last result to remove a problem. Firstly, they would try to 'educate' the person or people causing them the problem, making it clear that things had to change. If that did not work, then some serious intimidation would be employed. If that failed, then the only answer was a bullet in the back of the head.

These actions were well thought through. It was not anything personal, or done in anger. It would just be a bit of work, needed to protect the business and the operators of that business.

The true organised crime business is still operated by businessmen and criminal organisations such as the Mafia, Triads and South American drug cartels. They operate in much the same way as the organisational structure of a multinational company or government. All of these organisations – legal and illegal – have soldiers and enforcers, as well as penalties for breaking their rules.

Governments use police and armed forces to enforce their laws, and the courts to mete out the punishments. If you break their rules, you can expect heavy prison sentences.

The organised crime industry maims and terrorises people who get in the way. The death penalty still exists in that world, and there is no appeal system if the offender does not agree with his sentence.

Organised crime is normally a microscopic version of what civilised countries did in the past. Take drug dealing, prostitution, people trafficking and child-labour sweat shops. Governments of many countries have been involved in dirty deeds for generations. What about the slave trade, and the little children nowadays working in horrific conditions for high-street designer stores?

Britain turned China into a nation of junkies. Yes, we traded opium for tea after we acquired huge quantities of the drug from our activities in Bengal. The Chinese banned the drug in 1729 after a huge addiction problem. But in the 1830s Britain found a way around the trade ban and flooded China with opium. The Chinese hit back by capturing many of the traders and forcing them to hand over their opium. Britain responded by sending in the navy, including a new iron warship with a rocket launcher. We ran riot, killing up to 25,000 Chinese. Many of them were in a confused state, having become addicted to our opium.

Child labour was used in the rubber and sugar plantations to fill the coffers of the powerful nations in history. Prostitution was a business run since Roman times, if not before. To enforce these trades violence, intimidation and murder were used on a massive scale. All of these acts had the blessings of each country's rulers and governments.

Because of the availability of information on the internet and the aggressive press, governments and multinationals can no longer hide behind their veils of secrecy. More and more cases of corruption within governments and large companies are being exposed on a daily basis; one only has to look at our own politicians' expenses scandal, and the insider dealing and money laundering within our banking system.

MPs who had repaid their mortgages continued to claim thousands of pounds in interest. Just oversights, eh? Claiming interest for a non-existent mortgage? What about the guy who claimed more than £1,600 for a floating duck house? What about another one who claimed more than two grand to have his moat cleaned? Someone else claimed more than forty grand to furnish a small flat, while a lot of these claims were disguised. They were always 'flipping' their second homes to claim maximum allowances and generally taking the piss.

Why was a senior Tory trying to claim more than £15,000 in expenses to pay his daughter rent for a London flat ... even though he owned a home close to Westminster? When I read that another one had claimed £2,500 for treating dry rot at her partner's home, many miles from her constituency and Westminster, my faith in the system vanished. Shouldn't the whole lot of them have gone to jail? Would the man on the street be allowed to pay the money back and go unpunished? NO.

Things have reached such a state that people view politics as another form of organised crime. They call the House of Commons 'the House of Conmen' and the House of Lords 'the House of Frauds'. Who am I to argue with that?

The majority of the public don't trust politicians or bankers, and organised crime is now seen as not so bad after all! People say the lower classes are getting a better share of the cake by buying stolen goods that they would otherwise not be able to afford. If you talk to the average man on the street, most will say everyone is 'at it' – from the criminals on the street to the criminals in government and the heads of the multinationals. The working men and women believe they are the victims, paying for all of those luxurious lifestyles.

It's a sad state of affairs, because now we have the situation of who will guard the guards? The biggest con of all is this: if politicians or police get caught with their fingers in the till, who investigates them? The Police Complaints Commission and the Crown Prosecution Service are both government bodies ruled by Parliament. A mate of mine, former criminal Paul Ferris, summed it up nicely when he told me it was the same as asking Al Capone to investigate the Mafia. It's totally insane.

Not all politicians and police officers are bent – far from it. I have many good friends in both groups. But trust in these organisations falls away when one of their members gets caught breaking their own rules. It tars all of them with the same brush.

Honest politicians and police officers hate it when they find one of theirs has crossed over to the other side. It's the same as the organised crime business hating rapists, child molesters and grasses. So you can see that the crime business is not that far from a mini government, also having its own laws and codes of ethics and practices.

Crime, like everything in life, is evolving all the time. It doesn't stand still. Nature doesn't cater for voids. When a gang is taken out of existence, when you have a patch of weeds and they're taken out, other vegetation grows in. That applies to gangers and criminal businessmen.

While the gangsters are brawling in the pubs, criminal brains are checking out the latest security systems. As soon as one arrives on the market, criminal geniuses will find a way around it. Then a security company brings out another, more sophisticated system to keep robbers out. That one is studied in the greatest detail too, until a way is found around it ... and the evolution of crime goes up another step in the ladder, while the gangsters keep brawling.

Criminals with an eye for business are now experts in computer fraud, smuggling techniques and state-of-the-art weapons. If anything new comes out to give the business a boost, they will acquire it. They'll buy the thing and pull it apart.

Even as I write this, I'm reading about criminals – not gangsters – using 3D printers to develop weapons. It seems you can make plastic guns that fire live rounds. I imagine that a plastic gun would be a nightmare to detect at an airport.

Gangsters and businessmen on a local level will never get away with anything much today. Nowadays, if you want to get into crime, you have to be a head case. There is so much against you, including the police intelligence system. They can even trace your credit cards and see how you spend your money. The only people who do crime now are people who are really desperate to put food on the table. They usually have alcohol or drug problems, or mental health issues. The real organised criminals nowadays are sophisticated, like the police.

The crime business, though it may seem glamorous to the outsider, has a much darker side. It is full of nightmares and casualties and destroys the beauty of all we hold sacred in a civilised society. I was involved in a nightmare world with glitter thrown in to make it appear more desirable.

My realities began where other people's nightmares ended. The man in the street went to sleep with a dream under his pillow; I went to sleep with a gun under mine.

CHAPTER SEVEN
WOMEN, WOMEN AND MORE WOMEN

The activities of bad boys attract a certain type of female. These women dress sexily and are easily influenced and star-struck by the criminal's lifestyle. But they have little knowledge of how real organised crime operates, and are sucked into a world full of thuggery and illusions.

In my day there were set rules when you went out. You turned up at a pub or club, and your girl sat with her friends while the guys were left alone to talk about business. The females all knew each other. The girls discussed the new things we'd bought them or who was engaged or pregnant and all that. It was a pain in the arse if one of the guys was getting married. It meant that your woman would be on your back all the time about marrying her. That meant a lot of excuses, and even more expensive presents to shut them up.

Most were sensible enough to know what they could get out of you before you went to jail; then they would move on to the next crook. We called that type 'gangster groupies' and treated them accordingly. They were shag machines and just something you wore on your arm.

Then there was another type of real girlfriend who you had feelings for. Everyone knew that was your woman, and a definite no-go area for the other guys. I had a few of those relationships ...

I had a hippy girlfriend called Rosie, who was a weird but beautiful little thing. She was into flower power and free love and she had little flowers painted on her face. Rosie wanted me to be a hippy too so, to keep her sweet, I bought myself an Afghan coat and a headband. I looked the part when I took her to pop concerts and love-ins at Alexandra Palace.

The relationship didn't last long because I robbed the hippies of their drug money and beat up any guy who moved in on her. I wasn't cut out for the hippy life. Plus, Rosie was taking so many pills that she rattled as she walked, and the boys felt nervous around her. She did not click with the other girls because she wasn't into the money scene, so we just ended up as good friends.

Then there was June. Now she was beautiful, with loads of class, and was the only girlfriend who I respected and didn't sleep with. She came from Stoke Newington, or Stokie, which is in the Borough of Hackney in North London. Stokie has supplied the rest of the city with water from its rivers and reservoirs since the sixteenth century. And the place provided me with June. Even my mum liked her, and that was special for me.

One night I took her to the pub to meet my brothers and the rest of the firm. The guys were gobsmacked, seeing this swan amongst a bunch of pigeons.

'Where the hell did you get her?' Chrissie asked, trying not to look at her stunning figure. He was trying to catch sight of her legs, but this conservatively dressed beauty was showing only a glimpse below the knee.

'Look at that hair,' Neil said, wide eyed, as her shiny brown mane flowed perfectly down her back. A tiny black band held it all in place and just added to June's perfect lines.

'Look at those gorgeous brown eyes,' Old Frank whispered, trying not to sound jealous.

'She hardly wears any make-up,' my brother Frankie said, leaning over to catch Tony the Greek's attention.

'She doesn't need to wear any,' Tony told him, as this elegant young lady walked gracefully to the toilets and back, looking totally gorgeous.

Unfortunately, I wasn't a reliable boyfriend. I was always out with my mates, up to no good, while she stayed in a lot at her home. My God, she was loyal. When I got nicked for manslaughter, that girl wrote to me every week through the sentence, and I fell deeply in love with her. Up until that point, the only person who'd been loyal to me was that jewel in my crown, my mother.

I had a little picture of June on a board in my cell. One day a prisoner called Nicky, who was inside for GBH, came into my cell to talk about prison stuff. He looked at June's photo and said, 'She's a bit hot, you lucky bastard. I wouldn't mind giving her one myself.'

I saw red, jumped off the bed and battered him all around the cell. They could hear him screaming on the landing.

Terry, who was in the next cell, came running in, shouting, 'Stop it, Bobby! The screws are coming!'

I had my fingers in Nicky's eye sockets and was trying to pull his eyes out; I was determined to blind the bastard for looking at her that way. I was taken down the block to solitary for fighting, but after that nobody ever made crude remarks about her again.

June met someone near the end of that sentence and we parted. Everyone thought, after my release, that I would go and get her back, but I never did. June was not cut out to be involved with a criminal. I wanted to hang on to that memory, because all that faced me was a world of brutality and nightmares. Even to this day I respect her and I know that she was something decent and pure in my life.

When I wasn't banged up in the detention centre or in prison after the manslaughter sentence, I went from one girlfriend to another. After all, I had to go without sex for years, and so when I was out I was at it like a fucking rabbit on heat. We all changed our girlfriends on a regular basis, because you couldn't allow yourself to get too involved. At some point, you knew you would be going to jail for a long time and you couldn't expect a woman to wait for all those years and be faithful. If it was the other way round, you wouldn't be sitting at home knitting while she did her bird. Also, if you were on your toes – on the run – a real relationship was more of a liability than an asset.

In that world, relationships would appear to be good on the surface but underneath they had no solid foundations.

Balbriggan
Library
Ph: 8704401

All of us were on the hunt for a pretty woman, but things didn't always turn out the way we had intended, as Chrissy the Greek found out to his cost in the Hercules pub one night.

He and Andy the Greek thought they were God's gift to women and, to be fair, they were always well turned out. If a girl just looked at them, they automatically thought she was in love with them, as was the case in the pub that night.

I was with my girlfriend at the time, having a laugh with the boys, when Chrissy said to me that he reckoned a woman sitting near us fancied him. Needless to say, Andy thought the same and they were both preening themselves, trying to catch her attention.

The lights were dim – the same as any other club or pub, so you couldn't see the dirt and grime on the surroundings (if you saw the inside of most nightclubs in the daytime, you would never drink in them), but I could just make out that she had false-looking blonde hair, a low-cut top and plenty of bling: there were long earrings, bangles, gaudy rings and all that. The short skirt just covered her thighs, showing shapely legs all the way down to high-heeled, open-toed sandals that revealed bright red painted toenails. Tarty or what.

We watched the two Greeks swing into action. In a flash, those two dirty bastards were on either side of her. I noticed that she had a massive guy with her – obviously a minder – and he looked as if he'd been through a few wars. I imagined that he could handle himself.

I called Chrissy back and told him, 'You be careful there. She obviously has a few quid, with all those sparklers around her neck. She's a high society bird, out looking for a bit of rough.'

Even though I marked Chrissy's card that she had a minder with her, he said that he 'was well in there' and that she loved him. Shortly afterwards, he disappeared with her and Andy came back sulking because his mate had scored and he'd had no luck. Within minutes, though, Andy had found another piece of skirt.

A few hours later it was closing time at the pub, and the place closed, but we always got 'afters'. Around midnight, there was this frantic banging on the door and I told Big Eddie to investigate.

He went to the door, opened it, and Chrissy came barging in as white as a ghost, looking dishevelled and petrified.

Eddie, Old Frank, Andy and Tony the Greek just stared and stared at him.

I wondered if he'd had a rough session with the bird – encountered her old man, or had a row with the minder. I thought Chrissy might have stabbed the minder, because he always carried a blade. If he had, I reckoned that was all we needed – the Old Bill pulling us in for a murder or a GBH over Chrissy shagging some old tart.

I told him so, but he said something else had happened; he was shaking like a leaf.

'You haven't nicked her sparklers, have you?' I quizzed him.

'No, there was none of that,' he gasped.

'Well then, what the fuck is going on?' I demanded.

'We knocked back a few vodkas ...' Chrissie said, looking a bit sheepish.

'And?' I urged, desperate to get to the bottom of things.

'It wasn't a woman. The "she" was a man.'

We all fell silent and gaped at Chrissy, waiting for him to reveal all.

We'd heard stories of this happening, but had never encountered any incidents in our manor or involving any members of our firm.

'She – or should I say he – took me back to a right posh place in Hampstead. We had a load of vodkas and one thing led to another. Everything seemed fine and we went into the bedroom, kissing all the time.'

'Get to the point,' I told him.

'She started to give me a blow job and I sucked her thru-penny bits.' He shuddered. 'Then I put my hand down her knickers, but there was no fanny down there. It was a big, hairy cock and she had a huge hard-on.'

'What?' We all shrieked with laugher.

'You're having us on!' I said, in between fits of mirth. 'And you were sucking the tits and getting a blow job! Come on, I'm not having that!'

'No, no, it's true! He or she, or whatever it was, jumped out of bed and put the light on. There was a wig on the dresser and I was looking at a geezer about fifty years old!'

Tony the Greek had to repeat everything twice, as usual: 'It was a fifty-year-old geezer! It was a fifty-year-old geezer! He had a big hairy cock! He had a big hairy cock!'

'Fucking hell, you got a blow job off an old geezer and you didn't know it was a bloke.' I grinned, stunned at the bizarre story.

'But she had a real woman's tits!' Chrissy pleaded. 'Please swear you won't tell anyone else.'

That was never going to stay quiet – Andy made sure it was the talk of the pub the next night. After that, every time Chrissy took a bird home he checked her private parts first. It meant Chrissy got a reputation as a dirty bastard and a pervert, so I suppose he couldn't win.

All our women were clued up not to say anything to anybody about what we did for a living. I remember I'd been dating a girl in Finchley for a few months. One night, I planned to take her out for a meal and on to a club afterwards. She asked me to pick her up at her house and meet her mum and dad for the first time. I said that was no problem, and agreed to turn up at eight o'clock.

Old Frank the driver took me to the house in a nice little middle-class street. I knocked on the door, Kathy answered and invited me in.

She was just finishing getting ready, which always pisses me off. To this day, I've never met a woman who gets ready on time. You always have to hang around for at least half an hour.

Needless to say, her mum was in the kitchen, cooking the old man's dinner. She offered me a cup of tea, which I dutifully accepted. Then the question came that all mothers ask: 'What do you do for a living?'

Now, wearing one of my best three-piece suits, I didn't look like a building-site worker. I didn't look like I collected the rubbish and I was far better suited and booted than any club doorman.

'I'm in banking,' I lied, thinking quickly.

As it happened, that didn't seem to be much of a lie: I collected money, paid out a lot of money and collected bad debts. So you can see where I'm coming from.

'That's a good job,' Kathy's mum said. 'Is it good pay?'

'Yes,' I lied again. 'We have a good bonus system, so the money's good.'

Desperate to move the conversation away from my occupation, I asked what she did for a living.

'I don't work,' she told me proudly, in a £5 accent, sounding posh. 'I'm a housewife. My husband has a good job as a police inspector.'

I nearly choked on my tea.

'Are you all right?' Kathy's mum asked, looking concerned as I spluttered and gasped for air.

'Yes, I'm OK.' I gulped. 'The tea went down the wrong hole.'

So an inspector in the Old Bill was coming home to dinner, I was taking his daughter out on the town to meet all my villainous friends, and Old Frank the driver was outside in his dodgy, high-powered motor.

Kathy had never mentioned that her dad was in the Old Bill. They were the last people in the world I wanted to upset, for obvious reasons. I was up shit creek without a paddle, and needed to get out of there fast.

When Kathy came downstairs, I thanked her mother for the tea and made a hasty retreat for the front door. Kathy followed, and must have been wondering what was going on.

'Just drive,' I said to Old Frank.

'You all right?' he asked.

'No, I think I'm coming down with a tummy bug. I'll see if I can eat something. Take us to that Indian place we went to last week.'

As soon as we arrived I had a bite to eat, said I was feeling worse, and told Kathy I felt really sick, which wasn't a lie. I told Old Frank to drive her home and I never saw her again.

After that, I made a point of always asking my girlfriend at the time what her parents did for a living. I have nothing against going out with a copper's daughter, but it's not on if you're a criminal.

In those days we did respect our women. No one in our firm ever beat up a woman. Nowadays, there's a big increase in females getting slapped about because guys disrespect them. They see it on the box. It's the culture now, and it's imported from America. It seems like when it all happens over there, a few years later it kicks off in Britain.

A beautiful woman is now the shining light in my life, and that guiding, brilliant light is my fantastic wife, Ami. I spent a long time looking for the right one. Eventually she came along, and I never looked back.

CHAPTER EIGHT

KILLING FOR CASH

There is no human or personal feeling in the crime business. Nothing.

When I was active, I would make known to all concerned: 'It doesn't matter whether I like you or hate you. It's nothing personal. If I'm paid to shoot you, I'll fucking shoot you because you are just a bit of work.' Anyone who crossed my firm knew that they risked anything from a gun butt smashed in the face, to wounding, to a whole lot worse.

At the peak of my powers I was tough and uncompromising but as fair as I could be. I rewarded loyalty and went to the ends of the earth to punish anyone who grassed on me.

I ruled my manor in North London with ruthless efficiency, enforced lucrative protection rackets and stalked the streets with that sawn-off, double-barrelled shotgun called Kennedy. That menacing weapon took no prisoners, and the sweaty, shitty smell of fear was a familiar tang in my nostrils. I was an evil bastard and, yes, I knew all about the contract killings that were going on.

When people are prepared to kill for a living, it's just their job. It's the same as a drug dealer. It doesn't matter whether he likes you or not. He sells the drugs to you because you're not a person; you're a £50 note.

There have been so many contract killings over the years that I've lost count, but let me just recap on one infamous incident. A businessman called Mohammed Raja was in the process of suing a landlord over a business deal. Mr Raja was stabbed and shot dead one night when he answered the door of his south London home. Two men were jailed for murder, and the landlord was jailed for manslaughter. They had been hired to attack the businessman, but had they, in fact, just been trying to frighten him?

The landlord's conviction was quashed by the Court of Appeal, and a legal wrangle followed over a financial settlement. The landlord was ordered to pay £6 million to the victim's family in a civil case. Contract killings can be hard to prove!

Before a contract killing, the assassin has to think: 'We have a rat here, and we need to get this rat sorted. All we are doing is getting rid of vermin.'

The key thing is that the victim has to be dehumanised and not seen as a person at all. He has to be viewed like that because, if you killed a person, you would forever be thinking about his family. He is simply a target, to be eliminated for cash.

Guns were the main weapons in my day, but death could also be delivered by other means. Cars were used, with clever drivers at the wheel. Knives and ice picks were effective. Sometimes the methods of choice involved a polythene bag over the head or a length of string for strangulation. It all depended on access to the victim, the location and all that.

It's not just about violence, because organisation and skill are also vital ingredients. You can pick up a thug from the street, but you can't train him to be a hitman. Thugs are thugs. Only a tiny percentage of the population has what it takes to be a hitman.

Contract killing is glamorised. You're a god, killing for cash, because you decide whether someone lives or dies. You have that power; you have the power of life and death.

There are so many myths; I know the truth.

Organised execution is carried out by people who are trained with a weapon, just as a clerk is familiar with a pen. In my day, the hitman was a highly trained person. We played by the rules. There were certain codes that you had to obey; things that you could do and you couldn't do. If you were given a target, you couldn't shoot him in front of his wife and kids, because you wouldn't want to be whacked in front of your wife and kids.

You would be sent somewhere and trained with the gun to be used for the kill. Normally, an ex-army person trained you with that weapon so that you didn't hurt innocent people. Then you would go out with someone else on a job. You didn't know the person you went out with, so you couldn't grass on each other.

If you messed up he would let you have it anyway, and you knew that.

You didn't want some lunatic firing the gun. A weapon might pull to the left or the right and you had to cater for that. If you were hired to shoot someone in the leg, the last thing you wanted was the gun to jump and end up shooting him in the chest, killing him. More often than not, you were there to perform a punishment exercise, such as kneecapping, and not an execution.

Sometimes you would go out and just stick a gun in the person's mouth, or kneel him down by a ditch and fire the weapon into the ground as a warning. If he didn't get off the manor he knew someone else would be coming soon, ready to place a bullet in the back of his head.

The army veterans were recruited into the criminal underworld when they retired. We paid better wages than alternative employers. Money has that power. It also meant that the legal forces, sent out to stop killings, were up against the best in the business.

You had to learn about various types of weapons and be able to use them, as you couldn't use the same weapons all the time: coppers would suss your MO (modus operandi) – method of working. You had to be able to vary your weapons. You read about other hits, and trials where people had been caught. You read books about how people had been assassinated. What evidence did they leave behind? Why were they caught? It was all a study of your job.

Revolvers were always used, rather than automatics. An automatic spits out spent cartridges whereas a revolver keeps them in the chamber, and that is what you want. You don't want to be bending down on the floor looking for spent cartridges as they can provide DNA for the forensics people, so an automatic is a non-starter.

You also needed a profile on the target, in the same way as intelligence services did their homework. You looked at things like their age and criminal contacts – you didn't want to be talking to someone who knew this guy. What made him tick? What was his routine? What did he like and not like? What time did he go to work or take his dog for a walk? Planning had to be perfect.

Your target's patterns were noted down and weak areas identified. You were looking for a time and place when there were no witnesses. The person had to be isolated, allowing the execution or punishment to take place.

People who do these things are not mindless thugs. There is so much to it that, if you were a moron, you couldn't do it.

The aim of a successful hit was to make sure it stopped gang warfare – and it did actually stop gang violence.

Our way of thinking was: *'We have a problem. Some of these crime families could blow up here. We don't want it to get out of hand. So it's best that we eliminate the cause of the problem.'*

You would be contacted to see if you were up for a bit of work. It could only be given to you by someone who was known and respected in a firm. You would know that person's background, sometimes going back as far as three generations. And you knew that if the police got hold of that guy he would be banged up, but would never grass on you.

In a typical, discreet killing in the 1970s, the death was made to look like an accident. No one suspected murder.

After all, when you kill someone you don't want it to appear like a hit, and get the coppers all over it. So, you might know that your target is a diabetic. He could have an accidental overdose of insulin, go into a coma, and it looks like natural causes. Who else would have given him an injection? That is how it worked. And look at lethal injections with poisons. What about the KGB? They did their work with umbrellas injecting people and all that. If it looks like a heart attack or other natural causes, then all the better – aggro from the police in those cases is minimal.

In my day, when a message had to be sent out to other firms – usually because someone had overstepped the mark – then a more public execution took place. A motorbike or a car would pull up in a busy street, the killer putting a bullet in the back of a man's head. Or someone would be dismembered and body parts left all over the place.

Occasionally, if one firm wanted to send a message to a firm that had caused aggravation, they would kill one of the gang members and send out either a hand or the eyes. They sent the eyes because they could only belong to the one person – a hand could have been nicked from a hospital or mortuary or somewhere like that. The eyes told the brutal truth.

In extreme circumstances, I've heard about the Colombian necklace being used. The target's throat would be cut, with the tongue brought out through the neck. That is still a popular method with drug cartels. Those cartels are also lethal with chainsaws, sawing people up in the bath while they are still alive.

When we heard about the Jill Dando killing, we knew straight away that it wasn't a professional hit. We wouldn't kill anyone in the media because of the outrage it causes, so they're safe. Same as you wouldn't hit a copper. You don't go shooting policemen unless you want a lot of aggravation. You'd have to be an absolute maniac to shoot a copper.

The value of life has changed dramatically since I was involved in crime. Now, we have lunatics on the street who'll do it for five grand so they can buy a bit of smack or whatever drugs they're on. They think it's cool. They read crime books which glamorise everything. They all want to be the man with the gun.

It's always been easy to get hold of a gun. You can even just get a replica and have it converted into a lethal firearm for a few quid.

If you go out with a gun always remember that, when people come looking for you, they will have a weapon. You will die a violent death if everything catches up with you. It might even come to the stage where you might have to top yourself. You can get to the stage where it is time for you to go. Do you want to do a life sentence with a thirty-year recommendation, living in a stinking cell for the rest of your life? Or do you have a nice bottle of champagne or brandy, enjoy a nice meal, then put a gun in your mouth and pull the trigger?

You can't go out shooting people, killing people and all that, if you're not prepared to go the whole way for yourself.

When I first became involved with guns it was a strange feeling. It's quite shocking to look back at it. If my children came up to me now and said, 'Dad, I've got a gun,' I would be horrified. I just can't imagine them going around with guns the way I did.

The change in criminal society happened when the drug culture started coming in. There is a vast amount of money to be made from it. It started off with a load of hippies just enjoying the feel-good factor and love-ins and flower power and all that. Then organised crime saw that there was money in it, and some rivals had to be eliminated.

Upper-class people enjoy cocaine at their parties. It's lovely, just having their friends around and enjoying a nice evening. They don't know what happens further down the chain. The money they're spending goes on illegal money lending. It goes on bringing illegal weapons into the country, violence on the street and protection. The upper-class cocaine users don't realise it, but they're helping to build up a criminal empire.

Eventually, their money helps to pay for someone's execution.

Outside the criminal culture, there are no feelings for anyone else. Victims of a contract killing don't count. It's not personal. If they get in the way and get shot, or they want to have a go at you and you shoot them, it doesn't matter. They're a bit of work. You're paid to shoot other villains. It doesn't matter if you like them or don't like them.

Back in my day, hitmen were paid a certain amount of money to blow someone's leg off – that was what they did for a living. And they killed for a fee without as much as a second thought.

It was all about the money. Nothing else mattered.

CHAPTER NINE
END OF FREEDOM

By the mid-1970s I was one of the country's most wanted men, with a colourful career in the business of crime behind me. I was back in action, big time, after the manslaughter disaster. I was also under pressure, trying to keep the firm running while the Old Bill tried everything to get me off the streets.

I heard that they were going round, talking to their 'snitches'. They camped at the scenes of crime, working out what was rumour and what was fact. They went around talking to people who handled or supplied guns. They were tapping phones and watching houses; they took pictures to see who went in and out. That police intelligence was spot on – I have to give them 10 out of 10 for that. There was a lot of rumour about what I was doing at the time and they pressed hard for the truth. I still managed to stay a step ahead as they gathered their evidence.

In fact, they just pulled me in once, while they looked for proof. I was charged after a complaint from a guy who said he'd been kidnapped over the disappearance of the Japanese Instrument of Surrender.

This was a priceless historical document. The Americans had a copy, the British had one, and the Japanese had the other.

The Old Bill said a cleaner had taken it from the Japanese Embassy and sold it on to someone else. The police then said that I kidnapped this 'someone else' and made off with the document. They said I sold it to the American Mafia because I'd come across them in prison during my manslaughter sentence. The story went that the document ended up in the hands of a dealer in America. I was charged with armed robbery, kidnap and endangering life.

Evidence was flimsy, to say the least. I stood trial at the Old Bailey and was found not guilty.

On leaving the place, I went into the Wig and Pen pub and the firm were all there. The coppers were having a game of darts, and one of our boys walked up and wiped the scoreboard. He wrote: 'Robbery Squad 0 / BC 1.'

The coppers were really pissed off about losing the case. My solicitor came over for a drink and said, 'If I were you, Mr Cummines, I would go overseas and not come back for a very long time. The word around here is that they are going to severely nick you.'

By that time I had done so many armed robberies that I thought if I was going to get nicked I may as well carry on. I reckoned that if they found out about one bit of work, they would find out about all the rest.

I was a man under extreme pressure. And the Old Bill still wouldn't leave me alone. Finally, instead of keeping an eye on me, they decided they needed to ask me a few questions. That was the word on the street, so I made myself scarce.

Sure enough, my picture appeared everywhere, and I had to be extra careful. The armed robberies continued, but I had other pressing matters on my mind. My dad was ill in hospital suffering from a brain tumour. He was in his seventies, but I'd thought he would still have plenty of life ahead of him.

I sneaked into the hospital with my brother Frankie, and I was lucky to get inside. The Old Bill was everywhere. I believed that they weren't going to nick me – they were going to shoot me.

I caught the attention of a tiny dark-haired nurse, who realised who I was straight away. She showed me a photo of myself and said, 'We were told, if you came here, to call the police straight away.'

I opened up my coat, showed her a .45 revolver and warned, 'If you phone them there will be a lot of dead and injured people in here.'

'OK, do us a favour then,' she said, with a cute smile. 'Here are a couple of patients' gowns. Could you and your brother put them on?'

I shook my head as the bizarre situation unfolded: two armed robbers strutting around in silly-looking gowns? Anyway, that's what happened and we roamed around the hospital wearing them.

Most of the time, we just stayed with our dad and talked to him. He was drifting in and out of consciousness, so we couldn't have a conversation with him; we just told our dad that we were there.

After three days our mum appeared and told us: 'Go away and get cleaned up and have a shave. I'll sit with him.'

We needed a break, really, and Frankie said he needed a pint. We found a local pub. Frankie had his pint and I had my usual bitter lemon.

As we sat in the corner, working out how to get back into the hospital, the pub door flew open and our niece ran in.

'I thought you might be in here,' she said with a sob. 'Your dad has gone.'

I was heartbroken. I hadn't had the chance to say goodbye. It was as if he'd waited for us to go, so he could be with Mum when he died.

Frankie went up to the bar and bought me a double vodka and lemonade. 'I know this is a one-off. Get that down you.'

Not long afterwards, still mourning my dad, a bright and sunny summer morning proved to be as grey a day as I can remember. The sun beamed down on that Sunday morning in 1978 – and the rest of the day proved to be even hotter.

I'd heard that the Old Bill were rounding up members of my firm; I'd heard that they were crashing into houses, looking for me again. I had to get out of the country, pronto.

I decided to stay in the Royal Scot Hotel at King's Cross under a false name until the heat died down. Sitting in my room, the phone rang and kept on ringing. No one was supposed to know I was there. After an hour or so of torture from it, I decided to answer it.

'Freddy here,' my brother said, sounding out of breath. 'They're really gunning for you this time.'

'Is that a joke?' I snapped. 'Well, I'm gunning for them as well. We can't talk on the phone. Come round to the hotel.'

I put down the phone and waited for Freddy. As I sat in the hotel room, flashbacks from my life filled my head. I'd been the centre of attraction wherever I went, but now I was the loneliest guy in the world. Still in my mid-twenties, all I could think was: 'Is someone going to grass on me? Is someone going to shoot me?' My world had no meaning. I had money and I had the accolades, but I had to live with myself, in that room on my own, because the Old Bill was looking for me.

There were only two ways that this was going to end: I was going to be shot dead, or I was going to do a lot of bird. Then I realised there was another option.

I thought, *'Fuck this,'* and I put the gun in my mouth.

I knew that if I was prepared to whack other people, I had to be prepared to do it to myself or spend thirty years in jail. And I didn't want to be buried alive in that concrete tomb. I was quite prepared to pop myself. I said earlier that, in my world, you had to be prepared to take your own life.

I felt the cold steel of the trigger. I took a last deep breath and closed my eyes. I thought about my family and friends, and everyone who had been so loyal to me all of my life.

The knock at the door came just in time. I put the gun down, opened the door and Freddy rushed in, bursting to give me updates.

'I'm being deadly serious, Bobby,' he spluttered. 'Most of

the boys have been nicked and it's only a matter of time …
you'll need an exit visa, and sharpish.'

Freddy was my eldest brother, with twenty years between
us. He wasn't really involved in our heavy jobs, but he was
an absolute diamond for sussing out the word on the street.
He knew who had been nicked, when they'd been nicked and
even had a guess at the likely charges.

He used to be a fireman, but had to give up his career after
being badly burned. We felt sorry for him, as he was just
doing odd jobs, and brought him into the firm. He had no
criminal record, so was ideal to ferry guns around for us.

I told Freddy my plan: 'I need to do some more work, and
then I'll disappear. The Bank of Ireland in Holloway Road
should do us nicely. I'll call on a few people from the manor,
if they haven't been nicked, and we can do a bit of work.'

'You need to get tooled up,' Freddy reminded me. 'Ernie
will sort you out.'

Ernie was ex-military and kept a substantial armoury in
his house. It was normal for us to visit him and add to our
collection of shooters.

Freddy continued: 'I put in your order for an Uzi. I don't
know much about those.'

'It's a sub-machine gun.'

'A machine gun?' Freddy laughed. 'Are you serious?'

'I'm deadly serious,' I said, with laughter the last thing on
my mind. 'It's compact and easy to maintain and repair. The
Israeli Mossad intelligence people used it. They're smooth as
silk to use.'

'Do the others know about the machine gun?' Freddy asked, growing more curious by the second.

'Well, I told Tony the Greek and he asked me if I was declaring war on society. But it's just a more efficient way of doing business.'

I didn't want to talk any more to Freddy about machine guns. I intended to concentrate on the difficult day ahead.

Freddy was the go-between, really, for getting me the gun, as he and Ernie were drinking pals and things had developed from there. Everything had been sweet, with no problems, and I assumed that normal service could be expected. Ernie had been a reliable tool merchant – supplier of weapons – and I guessed all was well.

'Let's do it,' I replied, trying to shake off any nerves about the day ahead.

As it happened, I had been due to collect a couple of hand guns – and the Uzi, if ready – from Ernie on that Sunday morning, anyway, so Freddy and I grabbed a cab to the top of Ernie's street, which was just around the corner from the Enkel Arms.

Everything seemed normal for a Sunday morning: an old lady collected milk from her doorstep; a couple of blokes had their heads under the bonnet of a rusty Cortina; and a group of stray dogs sniffed their bits and prepared for foreplay.

I wasn't prepared for what happened next.

We walked up to Ernie's door and I pressed the bell with my usual three rings to let him know it was me. I couldn't wait to see and feel the Uzi sub-machine gun.

If you watch those American TV cop shows you'll know exactly what to expect. All hell suddenly broke loose. A SWAT team – all in their intimidating outfits – surrounded us, pointing their machine guns and shouting at the tops of their voices.

It turned out afterwards that the police thought I would shoot at them, which explained why they were so heavily tooled up. Why did someone say that? Firing a gun at the Old Bill is the same as signing your own death warrant.

'Keep your hands where we can see them or you will be shot,' a stern voice yelled.

'Don't make any sudden moves,' I whispered to Freddy. 'They're serious. They'll shoot.'

'Lie on the ground,' the SWAT leader ordered, at the top of his voice.

'Fuck off,' I answered angrily, although I was in no position to argue. 'Can't you see I'm wearing an expensive suit?'

'Put your hands on the bonnet of that car,' he yelled, ignoring my concerns for the suit. 'I repeat – any sudden move and we will shoot.'

Freddy and I both put our hands on the warm bonnet of a police Volvo, which still had its blue lights flashing and engine running.

I have to say those guys were professional. Within seconds they had my jacket off and handcuffs on. I was searched from head to toe and, fortunately, had nothing to declare. Freddy endured the same treatment.

'You're nicked,' one of the formidable team yelled out.

When we were both sitting comfortably, the top-of-the-range Volvo whisked us off to Holloway nick.

As we drove along, I thought to myself: *'If my guys were trained like that, I could have robbed the Bank of England.'* Credit where credit is due: they were shit-hot at the kidnap game and lived up to their reputation as thief takers. I was just miffed that I was the thief being taken.

We just assumed that the coppers had had a tip-off. The possibility of being grassed up didn't enter our heads: that just did not happen inside a firm.

The next thing I knew I was in a cell at Holloway police station with a copper outside. He had instructions not to let anyone in apart from members of the SWAT squad. I was in there for hours. Freddy had a cell of his own, along with other members of the firm, but I was the main target.

As I sat there, I suddenly realised that I was the happiest guy in the world. It was all over. It was as if an enormous weight had been lifted off my shoulders. I was happy because it had ended. I'd been living in a whirlpool of insanity, not knowing where I was going. I'd been just a machine doing the business.

By the time I was nicked, in that instance, I'd lost myself; I'd lost my own personality. I was paranoid, totally paranoid. Everywhere I went, I had guns around me. I even had guns under the bed – pump-action shotguns and all that — and I seemed to have weapons everywhere.

I always wondered when an armed copper was going to whack me because I'd done a lot of armed robberies. I didn't want to be found in a gutter with a bullet in my head. I felt I was worth more than that.

I sat in the cell, feeling that my arrest had been a blessing in disguise.

I also knew that someone else would take my place on the manor, that even younger businessmen would take up our roles. And I thought: *'Just let them.'* The trouble with some people involved in villainy is that they don't know when to let go.

I reckoned that my time was up. I'd been 'at it' since primary school, served a spell in a detention centre for possession of a sawn-off shotgun, endured five years inside for manslaughter, and now faced a much longer stretch.

As all of those thoughts packed my head, a detective inspector and a sergeant came into the cell. 'Nice to see you, Bobby. Come with us and let's have a talk.'

I wasn't expecting those guys to be so nice! I walked into the interview room while all my crimes raced through my head. What did they have on me? Which mistakes had I made? Did they know about this robbery or that robbery? Were they going to charge me?

The DI sent out for cups of tea and offered cigarettes around while I sat and just looked at them, saying nothing.

The DI broke the silence: 'Bobby, you have been well active and I'm going to send you down for at least thirty years.'

'I've heard that one before,' I answered, imagining that his evidence was thin, as usual.

'I know,' the DI countered as his expression suddenly turned grim and he leaned forward. 'But this time I have you fucking bang to rights. I have a statement that puts you well in the frame and a member of your firm is willing to testify.'

I tried not to change my expression and stared straight back at him. What was he on about? Member of my firm? I said nothing.

'I don't have to give you any verbal or fit you up,' the DI continued. 'I'm going to play this right by the book because I have you now. I really do have you now.'

I decided to remain silent. I really couldn't see anyone in the firm talking.

He put his hands on the table, gave me a deep frown and continued. 'Just to show you good faith, like a condemned man, you can have your clean clothes and your aftershave brought in. You can even order your own takeaway so that you don't have to eat our canteen shit, and the taxpayer doesn't have to foot the bill.'

I almost winced as he laid it all on the line, but I still managed to remain expressionless.

'Even your bird can come to visit you, Mr Cummines. No matter what you do or what connections you have outside, nothing is going to help you. One of your firm is singing like a canary. We have other evidence, too. We have the guns, dates, times, places and faces. We know when you did each bit of work and it's all watertight. So please enjoy your stay with us.'

What could I say after that little lot? It wasn't worth uttering a word because, according to them, I'd been stitched up good and proper.

I was escorted back to the cell and left on my own again. However, true to the copper's word, my girlfriend, Valerie, appeared, a bit later.

'You all right, love?' I asked, straight away.

'Yes,' she answered, as her eyes welled up with tears. 'But they've been to our house and they took photos of things. They took some of your clothing and all that away, but said I could bring in your change of clothes, fags and toiletries.' She paused for breath and gave me a solemn look. 'There's something else.'

'Oh?' I asked, wondering what else could lie in store after such a horrific series of events.

'They said you're going away for thirty years.'

'They're talking absolute bollocks,' I heard myself hissing. 'They said that just to frighten you. They have nothing. We've been here before and I've walked away. Who else has been nicked this time?'

I was taken aback as she rattled off a list of names. Everyone in the business of armed robberies seemed to be on that list. The names even included people on the fringes, who'd supplied hideouts.

It was looking like the work of a grass, after all.

I started to become really concerned. What unnerved me most was the way the coppers were behaving. They were acting like gentlemen, not threatening to bang up wives or have kids taken into care. They weren't trying to do deals, and weren't trying to give me a load of verbal rubbish. It could mean only one thing. Those bastards did have it all in the bag, and my fucking party was truly over.

I kept wondering who the grass could be.

After the coppers had charged me with a long list of armed robberies, one of them said, 'There are people here who think that the Japanese document job was too big for you. I always thought you did it. Will you tell me?'

I just smiled at him.

Just before we went to court, my brief told me: 'Bobby, you're not going to walk away from this lot.'

Those words were all he needed to say. He was no mug and he had already got that earlier murder charge reduced to manslaughter. He'd also successfully defended me on several armed robbery charges in the past. When he told me about my desperate plight, I knew the Old Bill had fucked me good and proper.

We appeared at Highbury Corner Magistrates' Court for the charges to be read out and pleas taken. There were so many of us that they processed us in lots of four. Of course we all pleaded not guilty.

Standing in the dock with me was my brother Frankie, Old Frank the driver and Neil. I asked them if they were OK and if they knew who the grass was, but at that stage nobody had a clue.

We were remanded in custody at Brixton prison until the next hearing. I was placed on a different wing for a time, as

I'd been booked as high security. That was a real pain, as it meant I had a screw following me everywhere I went. He wrote everything I did in a little book; he even took notes about how many times I went for a shit. My clothes were kept outside my cell, as some sort of security measure, and a red light stayed on in there all night.

It was a great relief when they finally allowed me to mix with my brother and the rest of the firm.

During another appearance in court, my brief told me he had seen all the statements and that I would receive a copy.

'Who is the grass?' I demanded to know. 'Who is the fucking rat?'

My brief looked away, because he knew that to grass in our world was to plumb the very depths of the sewer. But that's not the way his sort thought or spoke. 'If you mean who is the prosecution's chief witness against you...' He took a deep breath, looked straight at me and said, 'It was Ernie.'

I felt my face twisting with hate. All the work we'd done, all of the conversations we'd had, all the planning and all of the raids. The bastard had told them everything!

Ernie was a marked man from then on, but we also heard that his family was on police protection around the clock. How were we going to get to Ernie and persuade him to change his statement?

The grim truth was that the Old Bill had already interviewed Ernie, before our arrival at his house, and obtained exact details about our operation. Ernie had told them all about my activities and really stitched me up. He had chapter and verse on my armed robberies and sang like a canary – just as the copper said. The Old Bill had heard about Ernie's firearms and explosives; he decided to tell all and make a deal for a shorter sentence.

I muttered to myself that I'd never been happy with Ernie. He used to buy drinks and all that, but I'd always had a gut feeling about him. I'd said to the others that I wasn't happy, but I had nothing concrete to go on so we'd kept dealing with him. Taking all of that into account, no one in the firm thought for one minute that he would spill the beans. You just don't do that when you work for a firm.

The only chance I had of getting near him was when we went to court, so I made a plan. I knew the prison officers had a routine where they brought me and the main parties up first, then some others behind us, and Ernie last of all on his firearms and explosives charges.

At Highbury Corner Magistrates' Court, on the day of our committal to the Old Bailey for trial, I made out that I needed to go to the loo. A court prison officer allowed me to use the toilets. I waited while my lot went up the steps, then the next lot, and then I heard Ernie's voice talking to the prison officers.

I waited until I could hear him coming, then I opened the toilet door and ran out and hit him square on the chin. He crashed into the wall and went down like a sack of potatoes.

As he lay there, I snarled, 'You will be my next bit of work.'

The alarm bell went and I had court prison officers all over me. I was pushed into a cell while they took care of

Ernie. About half an hour later the door opened again. The hallway was full of court prison officers and police. They put handcuffs on me and took me upstairs into the dock, which was empty except for the prison officers. My co-defendants were made to stand in front of the dock while I was handcuffed to the fucking thing and surrounded by guards.

I looked up at the public gallery; it was full. Everyone had noted that I was cuffed to the dock and surrounded by guards, and I could hear them all murmuring.

The magistrate then came in and asked if it was really necessary for me to be cuffed to the dock with so many guards surrounding me. The prosecution explained that I was very violent, that I had attacked one of my co-accused in the cells, and they feared for his safety. The magistrate agreed, and all the charges were read out. I faced thirteen counts of armed robbery, thirteen charges of possession of illegal firearms and thirteen of endangering life. Unlucky 13 or what! Add to that list fourteen counts of conspiracy and they had done me for the fucking lot. No stone was left unturned and, even worse, they had really done their homework with all the evidence to prove everything. Sadly for me, they'd got their numbers right, and I stood no chance.

The magistrate listened to the prosecution and defence statements and sent us for trial to the Old Bailey.

I sat in the dock and looked at my friends on trial with me. I knew each of them had families and all of us faced lengthy prison sentences. Everyone had been loyal and believed in me. The best I could do for them was a damage limitation exercise. I had always believed that 'Better one go than all of you', and I knew the one they really wanted was me.

We were all sent back to Brixton prison, and that night I thought up the plan. I sent a note to each of the firm telling them all to write their statements, pointing the blame my way and to do the best deals they could with the prosecution. We were going to be found guilty anyway.

Some of the guys were grateful, although they didn't like the idea of sending me up the river. I said I was gone anyway, thanks to the rat Ernie.

We sat in Brixton for nearly a year awaiting trial. Our families visited us every day and our briefs saw us from time to time to prepare for our trial, working out mitigating circumstances; in my case I had none, unless I wanted to plead insanity.

Eventually, the day of our trial arrived. All of us, except Ernie, were taken to the reception unit where we put on our suits to go to the Old Bailey. It was the first time for the rest of them, but of course I had been there before, when I was much younger, for carrying a sawn-off shotgun. I remembered that was when I'd met the Krays.

The old place reeked of history: not only the Krays' trial, but the Richardson gang trial, the Ruth Ellis case and a lot more. Many people had gone to the gallows from the Old Bailey. It was built on the site of Newgate prison, and centuries of pain and misery seeped through every brick in its cells.

I had a feeling of foreboding as we entered the building. The Statue of Justice weighed heavily against any villain who stood in its docks.

As they led us up the staircase that led to the dock, I could see my men looking at one another. They had no idea what to expect at the top of the stairs, but I knew the layout and didn't give a fuck. I'd seen it all before.

At the top of the stairs was the courtroom, with the judge and barristers dressed in their ritual garb as if ready to perform in some Shakespearean play. At the end of it all there would be a human sacrifice: us.

We all sat in the dock and the judge appeared. We were all told to stand up and sit down. I remembered a childhood song about standing up, sitting down and keeping moving and started to laugh.

'Do you find this funny, Mr Cummines?'

'No, Your Honour. It's nerves,' I lied.

I could see that comment was not believed, and I mumbled to myself, 'There you are dressed in stockings, wearing a wig and a red robe, and you expect me to take you fucking seriously.'

It was like looking at an old Jacobean transvestite. The difference was that this weirdo could send me to prison for thirty years, so I bit my lip. It was best not to wind up the beak too much.

Our family and friends sat in the public gallery, along with members of the public and law students. We made sure that our parents didn't attend. The evidence and all that would have broken their hearts, and I was happy that they weren't in court.

Everyone listened intently as the police gave their version of events. My name was mentioned more and more as the tales of villainy unfolded. They talked about intimidation, ruthlessness, dangerous people and disrespect for human life. The general tone went along the lines that Bobby Cummines was one bad bastard, by all accounts.

'Hear, hear,' I could imagine members of the Metropolitan Choir singing, now that they were nailing their man.

I just sat there looking up at my family and friends in the public gallery. My brother Frankie, Neil, Freddy and Old Frank, all in the dock, exchanged glances.

Then came Ernie, who sat in the dock smiling like a kid who had just won a goldfish at the fairground. He waved to me and said, 'Hello, Bobby, I didn't want to do you but they wanted you more than anybody else. I like you, really.'

'Are you taking the piss?' I barked back.

'No, I really like you, Bobby.'

'Well, I'm fucking glad that you don't hate me,' I snapped.

Everyone in the public gallery started laughing and the judge had to bring the court back to normality with the 'Silence in court!' stuff. He warned me not to use foul language in court, and then told Ernie to give his evidence about the armed robberies.

As expected, Ernie sang like a canary that had never sung before, describing how he'd supplied the guns for our escapades.

'I can get you anything. I can even get you a bloody tank if you've got the money.'

We sniggered in the dock because we knew Ernie was a nutter who worshipped weapons and explosives. He dressed up in American Civil War uniforms and had the Union flag above his bed – with a barrel of gunpowder beneath it. In fact, Ernie the Grass had enough explosives under his bed to blow half the street away.

The Old Bill shat themselves when they saw that lot and quickly got rid of it all.

When Ernie had finished giving his evidence, the judge said, 'I understand that you are under police protection. Do you really fear these men so much?'

'I'm not really worried about the others, but I am sure that Bobby would shoot me.'

'Thanks a lot, Ernie,' I thought. *'You've just added another five years to my sentence.'* The court was adjourned until the next day and we all went back to Brixton.

That night we went through the plan to blame everything on me. I said everyone should plead guilty, and I would say everyone did as I asked because they were afraid. I pointed out that there would be reduced sentences for guilty pleas, and we didn't want the victims in the witness box talking about their recurring nightmares – I knew that guilty pleas would avoid the need for witnesses. Graphic details from those sobbing, shaking witnesses, before sentencing, weren't going to help our cases. We all agreed that my plan was the only sensible and decent thing to do.

The next day we all appeared in court again. After we'd gone through the rigmarole of standing up and sitting down, I asked the judge if I could change my plea. I said I wished to address the court. Permission was granted.

'Your Honour, I feel it is only right to change my plea to guilty. I am guilty of all of these offences and, out of decency, I feel it would be totally wrong for the victims of these crimes to have to recount and relive their painful experiences.

'I wish to cause them no further pain. I do not ask for mercy, as I did not show any and don't deserve any. However, I would ask that you take into account, when sentencing my co-defendants, that they were my men acting under my instructions. If they had not done what I told them to do, I would have shot them. Thank you. That is all I have to say.'

I saw the judge sit up and raise an eyebrow. 'I accept your plea. Take him downstairs. I will sentence him later.'

After that, the judge listened as the barristers laid out their cases for lighter sentences, while I was described as a modern-day Genghis Khan.

The judge adjourned the case for three days before sentencing us. I told my girlfriend that I was expecting to get eighteen to twenty years, but only fifteen years if I was really lucky. The rest of the boys might expect ten to twelve, I reckoned.

I was the first up.

The judge narrowed his eyes and looked at me. He didn't mince his words. 'These crimes are of the most serious nature and deserve to be treated as such. You were no doubt the gang leader and the organiser of these crimes. During this trial, all I have heard is the name "Bobby Cummines", and yet there are twelve other accused in the dock with you.'

The judge was no fool and he really let me have it. 'I don't believe for a moment that they went and committed these crimes just because they were afraid of you.'

Quick as a flash, my barrister waded in and said I was kind to elderly people. He told the court that, in my local pub, I would buy their first drink and pay for their Sunday lunches. That was true, although I wasn't sure if generosity in the pub would convince the grumpy, glaring old bloke in the robes and wig.

The judge replied, 'I am sure he is a generous man. When you do what he does for a living, you can afford to be very generous, I am sure.'

My brief sat down, I took a deep breath and the judge stared at me again.

'I have taken into account that you changed your plea to guilty to save the victims having to relive those terrible events, and I believe that there is some humanity in you. I will reflect this in my sentencing. I will not give you the sentence I was going to give you. I will reduce it to twelve years. Take him down.'

That was a bit of a result. Twelve years on all counts, to run concurrently. It was so much better than I'd been expecting, as I'd already done all that earlier bird. The others received sentences of eight years downwards, depending on their involvement. Charlie Richardson was given twenty-five years of bird with his GBH charges for allegedly using his 'black box' torture treatment and all that, so I counted myself fortunate.

My destination: HMP Albany, on the Isle of Wight. High security for one of Britain's most dangerous men. There I was, in 1978, at the age of twenty-seven, about to lose the prime years of my life. The year 1990 seemed such a long way off.

The future looked grim. Very grim.

CHAPTER TEN

THE KRAYS AND THE RICHARDSONS – ALL TOOLED UP

Albany was a frightening, frightening place, where it was easy to lose all hope for the future.

I sat alone in my cell, wondering what lay ahead. I felt no remorse for any of my activities, apart from that accidental death during the armed robbery several years earlier. I thought that, generally, my actions were justified as bits of work. As I look back now, I can see that a lot of my activities were sheer lunacy. Much of what I did was total insanity. If I could turn the clock back ... who knows?

You have to remember that I was up against some really nasty people and they received what was coming to them. Of course, those villains had families and I feel sorry to have caused them so much grief. I suppose one silver lining is that because of my actions back then, I have a lot of credibility when I come to try to stop youth crime today ... so I have turned that negative into a real positive.

I scanned the scanty surroundings of the small cell. It must have been around twelve feet by six feet, with lino on the floor. There was a bed, a small table and not much else. The first thing I did was to hang a picture of the Queen on my cell wall. That tradition had stayed with me since childhood, and would never change.

The window was bigger than I was used to in prison, and I peered through the bars onto the exercise yard. It was a mass of concrete with not one blade of grass in sight.

I saw an intercom gadget on the wall and pressed the button. I asked the guard in his sealed office if I could go to the toilet and the door opened electronically: only one prisoner was allowed out of his cell at a time.

This was a high-tech prison. I even had a key to lock my door. Well, there was nowhere to go apart from the normal prison areas, so no one could escape, or anything like that. My convictions, including manslaughter, ensured that I always had a cell to myself and was kept away from other inmates.

I soon became used to the system. I went down for breakfast, mopped the landing, watched TV and made as many friends as I could. There were set times for meals, and these were cooked by the prisoners. The food was brought out on trolleys and you could eat them in the TV room. You could also eat in your cell if you wanted some peace.

My mum never came to see me – it would have been too much for her – but my sisters and friends came to Albany. It was difficult for them to get to the Isle of Wight, because the ferry didn't run in rough weather, and it took visitors all day to get there and back. Albany and Parkhurst were jails within jails.

I had heard that some of the Albany prisoners were receiving beatings. Everyone knew what was going on and we all refused to go back into our cells until the beatings stopped. The people in charge were making a pig's ear of running the place. I'd heard that 'snatch squads' were taking prisoners away and handing out terrible treatment. They were attacking prisoners who made their lives a misery by complaining about everything, from being locked up too much to the quality of the food.

I seized my chance to get my opinion heard when a group of prison staff went on walkabout on our landing. I confronted the gaffer: 'We want to see our people,' I shouted. 'They're receiving beatings. That's totally unacceptable, and we want to know what's going on.'

'Let me go!' he responded.

I bristled with rage, grabbed hold of him and ranted about the stories of beatings. 'You rat!' I spat out with venom. 'People are being taken down the block and abused.'

The governor assumed I had it in for him: 'He's taking me hostage!'

Well, he mentioned that word – not me – but the situation began to deteriorate.

With feelings running high on all sides the screws ganged up, and the other prisoners gathered around me. I held him by the front of his shirt and slammed him against the wall.

'I'm the governor. Don't you know I'm the bloody governor?'

I looked him straight in the eyes, tightened my grip, and

gave him a simple message: 'And I'm fucking violent!' It couldn't have been more straightforward.

That governor was far too cocky. But he knew that I meant business. One of the Irish prisoners slipped a blade into my hand.

I felt the chilling, smooth surface of the ice-cold metal. The head honcho's eyes bulged as I held it against his cheek; I felt him tremble. The screws didn't flinch. They stood like statues, gaping, and hardly believing that their boss was within an inch of his life.

Everything went quiet. Then a glass fell to the ground; a warder coughed; the governor carried on shaking. And I let him feel the point of the blade.

I had to carry on, as he had upped the ante. I was in an impossible situation. I couldn't let him go. The screws were all pent up, and I knew if I let him go they would have ripped me to pieces like a pack of wild dogs. They had all the reasons they needed by saying the governor had been taken hostage by a violent prisoner who had had to be restrained.

We were all aware at the time that there were deaths in prisons through the practice of restraint using body belts. These are belts that go around the body with fitted handcuffs: no way out of those. And they are still in use today.

I pushed my forehead into his face, as if preparing for a head-butt. 'You tell me why the screws have been kicking the shit out of my lads. Do that and I might let you go.'

Still, no one moved. The screws stood hunched in a circle, ready to pounce if I dropped my guard.

'YOU BASTARD,' I yelled in the governor's ear. I knew I had to make a decision. 'He's coming with me,' I announced to the assembled friends and enemies, sounding as menacing as possible. 'No one makes the slightest movement. Is that understood?'

They understood, and my brain raced to work out the next move. I was in deep, deep trouble and I sensed that things were going to get a lot, lot worse. I took the deepest breath I'd ever taken and marched along the landing with the governor of Albany Category A prison. He must have believed that his life was hanging by a thread.

I took the governor as far as my cell, turned him around, kicked him up the arse and threw him out. I closed the door and wedged it shut because the screws were ready to come in mob-handed. They left me in there for three days – their way of punishing me, I suppose. They were good enough to slide some rations into the cell so at least I didn't starve.

When the cell door finally opened – electronically, of course – after those painfully long days and nights, I saw a line of screws stretching all the way down to the prison van.

My punishment: long spells of solitary confinement. No one spoke to me, and my food was delivered to the cell door. They isolated me from everyone else.

After that, I was labelled 'the most subversive man in Britain' and 'the most dangerous person in the country'. Also, on my files, it said: 'He takes hostages.' Yes, I had very little going for me in the mid-1980s.

At that time Albany was a top-security jail, housing around 300 inmates. Albany was originally built as a Category C training prison in the early 1960s. The jail took over the site of a former military barracks.

Albany and Parkhurst, a short distance apart, were known as dispersal prisons. This meant that the country's most serious offenders would not all be housed together. They were kept at a small number of jails and could be ghosted to another dispersal prison at short notice. I was regularly moved between Albany and Parkhurst.

The staffing at Albany was around fifty when you included the governor and his people, admin, catering and warders. The idea was to reform and rehabilitate, so there were woodwork classes and all that. But it was a brutal system and I didn't see much rehabilitating going on.

Some men carried out maintenance work or had jobs in the kitchen. Others worked in the hospital wing, and a few guys kept the gardens tidy. I was kept away from the other prisoners and didn't get involved in the woodwork classes or odd jobs.

We were paid around £3 a week, as basic, which was used as credit at the prison shop. Prisoners who carried out work received a bit extra. The shop sold newspapers, sweets, orange juice, biscuits, tinned milk and all that. The milk tin lids came in handy as sharp, razor-type weapons to cut people with.

Nearby Parkhurst was a grim-looking place. It was built as a military hospital in 1805 and became known as Britain's Alcatraz. Boys awaiting deportation to Australia were held there.

Prisoners built a wing of the prison in 1847, and it was still in use during my time there. The inmates had dug the clay and baked the bricks themselves.

Many children who had stolen food to survive were kept at Parkhurst, in leg irons. Around 1863 this forbidding place became a female prison. After six years of feminine occupation, Parkhurst was converted to a male prison and that was how it stayed.

The next stop after Albany and Parkhurst was Broadmoor, if you had mental problems, as happened with Ronnie Kray. Violent but sane, I avoided that fate.

Despite being locked up, prisoners who had businesses on the outside were safe in the knowledge that their interests were still being looked after: their families stepped in to keep things ticking over, ready for their release date.

My distinctive business style was well known to other prisoners. On the outside, when someone wanted to do a deal with me, I put £1 and a bullet on a table. 'If you want to do business with me, there are two ways,' I used to say. 'If you carry out a straight deal, you will make lots of money,' I would say, pointing to the £1 coin. 'If you fuck with me you'll get that,' I would add with a snarl, pointing to the bullet.

On the inside I conducted business meetings, too … only then I made sure that I was tooled up with a blade in case things got out of hand.

The entire prison system, from top to bottom, knew that I could fix everything, from a smuggled steak to more sinister activities. It was best that people knew not to fuck with me. In a maximum-security prison, I learned brutality and the art of survival.

During one spell in Parkhurst, I got to hear that the Krays wanted to form a sort of gangster union. They were talking to the Mafia and getting ideas. Reggie said they were getting older now and they could be the Mustache Petes. The younger guys would be the Godfathers. Reggie believed that all the serious firms could form an Italian Mafia-style operation in England.

'Mustache Pete' was the name given to members of the Sicilian Mafia who went to America in the early 1900s, and the Krays liked the idea of being the 'old guard'.

Reggie was in Parkhurst with me and Charlie Richardson, while Ronnie Kray lurked menacingly in Broadmoor.

My first meeting with Charlie Richardson took me by surprise. Gary Wilson, Charlie's main man, came to see me and said, 'Charlie wants to speak to you.'

When Charlie Richardson wanted to speak to you, that is what you did.

As I went into his cell, I saw that he was immaculate. His shirt was ironed and his moustache was neatly trimmed. He also had many, many books in his cell, and he had huge piles of newspaper cuttings on his table.

'I've heard a lot about you,' Charlie said as I walked in. He looked me up and down with his questioning blue eyes. 'You're running the money lending in here.'

'That's right,' I said. 'I'm a fixer, really.'

I was maintaining a relaxed front, but inside I knew that I was chatting to the real deal; I was looking at criminal history.

'Have a cup of tea. Sit down with me.'

I sat down at the large table inside Charlie's cell and waited to hear what he had to say.

'You're too smart to be a thug,' he told me. 'You don't want to be a man with a gun. I'd like to see you again. Come and see me regularly. Come in every two o' clock and have a cup of tea and a bit of lunch.'

During those meetings, Charlie talked about straight business, which surprised me. He described how a lot of money could be made by staying on the right side of the law. I was all ears during those chats and learned a lot.

Charlie wasn't into making enemies. He preferred the 'Old English' way, where everyone had their own manors and they could all do business. He tried to keep people on his side, to see what they could offer him. If he was talking to another firm, he would check out their business to see if he could have a piece of it. Charlie always looked for the deal. The Krays hated what he was doing because they didn't have the brains for that. They had plenty of brawn, but that was about it.

In Parkhurst there was a prisoner, known to be an assassin, who came up to me. He said Ronnie Kray had sent a note down, from Broadmoor, instructing Reggie to sort out Charlie Richardson. Ronnie wanted Charlie whacked. I thought the messenger was having a laugh, because Ronnie Kray was totally off his head.

The letter read something like: 'I want you to fucking do Charlie.' The word got out that those who were loyal to Reggie were tooling up and those who were loyal to Charlie were tooling up, too. I realised that this could end up as a bloodbath.

By then I was running many of the businesses in the prison – everything from trading in gold rings to issuing personal loans. Because of all my deals, I had become heavily involved with Reggie and Charlie. I didn't want to lose either friendship. And I didn't want to lose my life, at barely thirty years old.

I went into Charlie's cell: our meetings had become part of my daily routine. He was having a puff, reading his news-paper and sipping a cup of tea. I told him that people were becoming paranoid. He asked me what I was talking about. I asked him if he had set someone up to whack Reggie – I suggested that Ronnie's letter could have been a pre-emptive strike.

Charlie hadn't made any moves at all; he said Ronnie was off his head and not to worry about it. I received Charlie's usual instruction: 'Fucking sort it out. Good boy, good boy.'

I went in to see Reggie. I told him that it could end up as a bloodbath. A lot of people were loyal to Charlie and, when it came down to it, I could not see Reggie winning.

'I'm not scared of Charlie,' Reggie told me.

'And he's not scared of you,' I assured him.

'Yes, I know that,' Reggie confirmed.

'So how about we have a compromise?' I suggested. 'The

way I'm looking at it, we could have firms cutting each other to pieces. We want to earn our little livings and get home to our families.

'It's all right for you. You've plenty of bird to do, but a lot of people are looking forward to going home and they can't be "true to two". They're going to have to take sides and you won't want to take responsibility for that. Many people will back you, but a lot will back Charlie, and you could end up dead here.'

If Charlie was whacked, people would get longer sentences and Reggie's reputation would go out of the window. The same would apply to Charlie, so there'd be no winners at all.

I said it was best if we sorted things out because we all had things as we wanted them inside. We had steaks coming in, along with whisky and dope. It was all sweet. Enough of the screws knew what was going on for the system to work and were quite happy with me being the prison fixer. They realised that my organisational skills, finely honed in the manor, had been transferred into the prison system. They just stayed away from me.

I went back to Charlie and he came up with a compromise. He said he would meet Reggie downstairs in a little room in the gym. The doors could be blocked off, and it would be sorted out there and then.

I reported back to Reggie with the offer about how the two of them could straighten things out. Reggie knew that he was trapped in a corner. Not only that, he had all his own rackets sewn up, too. Plus, he enjoyed his steaks, and he even had stars of the day, such as Barbara Windsor, visiting him. Ronnie was behind all the problems.

Reggie didn't take up the offer of a straightener, so I suggested that they should sort it out when they were released. He just said: 'Yeah.' I reported back to Charlie and his response was: 'Any time.'

When it all died down, the prisoner who had tipped me off looked over at me, keen to know the outcome.

I put up a thumb. He came over, gave me a little bottle of Irish whiskey and said, 'Thank you.'

Prison is a dangerous, dangerous place. It's even more hazardous when you come to the end of your sentence. People like to put you in a difficult position and they get a bit lippy. So you have the choice of taking them out and getting another big sentence, or just walking away and earning money on the outside. The top guys had the strength to bite their lip, walk away and leave revenge for another day.

I had to put up with the prison politics and a lot of bickering. The 'p' in 'prison' stands for paranoia. This is an environment where there is jealousy all over the place, especially if you are one of the main men. It's like a little-girls' school in that respect. And some of the people in there are pathetic. You have fifty-year-old men strutting around in boxer shots and trainers, trying to look nineteen. There they are, doing a ten-year stretch and trying to look like teenagers and copy the young guys. I've never understood why they do that.

Some of the screws had a screw loose, too. I remember a screw who was a chronic alcoholic. He used to give the boys a bit of tobacco, or anything, for a quiet life. He tried to be official but he was the worst screw in the world.

One Christmas Eve, he came into a cell where we were having a drink. We had all the booze out, with a collection of smuggled and homemade brews in buckets. I needed a break from my bitter lemons.

The screw said, 'Is that booze in there?'

Well, it was obvious that we had an assortment of booze in the buckets and all that, so he said, 'What does it taste like?'

The next thing we knew, he was sitting down on the bed having the booze with us. We made our own booze at all the prisons. We used to get the yeast and the potato peelings out of the kitchens to make hooch. Plus, we had bent screws in there who brought in bottles of whisky and all that sort of thing.

After a while, he remembered that the chief officer was due on the wing that night and, when we heard the heavy boots clattering along the corridor, we hid him under the bed. We concealed everything, pretended we were having a festive chat, and they didn't trouble us. He was still drunk in the morning, and the other screws only just managed to smuggle him home.

Well, the same screw was on duty one night when one of the guys had a headache after having a bit of puff. Some of the screws had gone to a local pub and they were well pissed by dinner time. This screw was supposed to call the medical officer and not give any medication, but he was so pissed that he couldn't be bothered. The screw went to his office and found a couple of tablets. He gave them to the guy, who drank some water and threw them down his neck.

'Help, help!' the prisoner said after a few minutes. 'I'm dying. I'm dying!'

This was serious. The bloke was screaming and trying to knock his door down. His medication had given him more than a headache.

Screws appeared from everywhere and rushed the guy off to hospital. It turned out that he'd been given water-purification tablets for the swimming pool and they had almost burned his gut away. The prisoner sued the authorities and the screw was pensioned off.

Who said prison was a cushy number?

CHAPTER ELEVEN

THE YORKSHIRE RIPPER AND FRIENDS

I was seen as such a dangerous prisoner that I was sent from Albany to Lincoln, Leicester, Bedford, Wormwood Scrubs, Wandsworth, Parkhurst, Maidstone, back to Parkhurst, Maidstone again, Birmingham … you name the prison, and I was probably sent there.

A dangerous man such as me, in the Category A bracket, with all my subversive tendencies, couldn't be allowed to grow roots in the one place.

You do feel unloved when even a jail doesn't want your company.

At the time, maybe, they had a point. When I had patrolled my manor in North London, though, I hardly expected to be rubbing shoulders with the Kray twins, Charlie Richardson and the Brink's-MAT robbers.

At Parkhurst and Albany, we were also housed in the same wing as the IRA, UDA and Colonel Gaddafi's special agent – a top man in the Libyan army – who shot a copper in Regent's Park. He had velvet curtains in his cell, plus his own butler, and an endless list of comforts sent by the colonel himself. Gaddafi's people provided him with everything he wanted. His family was flown in, and he even received his salary. One day he vanished out of the system, and then he sent Charlie Richardson a card from Libya. He'd been exchanged for a prisoner over there.

I could cope with all of the above because they were straightforward people, however brutal, and you knew where you stood with them. We all detested the fact that scum like child-killers were in the same prison as us. They had to be kept in a special unit – the Vulnerable Prisoners' Unit – for their own safety; believe me, we would have torn them to pieces.

IRA, UDA and other terrorist groups kept very much to themselves; the drug cartels stuck to their own people; and the armed robbers and other criminals also kept themselves to themselves. Domestic killers and oddballs had their own groups.

My old man used to say: 'If it walks like a duck, talks like a duck, and is seen in the constant company of ducks, then it is quite obviously a fucking duck.' His phrase was an ideal description of the various groups of prisoners.

Because of our confined living space, though, we crossed paths and socialised with other factions, apart from the bastards in the VPU. In prison you have nothing, really, apart from your self-respect and the bonds you can form with people. But there is a hierarchy from top to bottom – which comes as a surprise at first.

At Albany, I was walking around the exercise yard with

my friend, Eddy (no relation to our mountainous minder), who was serving life for murder.

'Look at those fucking nonces,' he growled loudly, staring at two prisoners in the VPU, who were talking through their windows. 'If I get my hands on the bastards, as God is my witness, I'll cut off their bollocks.'

'Harsh but fair,' I agreed, watching them having a cosy chat through the wire-covered barred windows. The wire was there to prevent us throwing bricks into their cells.

The two targets of Eddy's abuse looked shocked. One of them, a weedy character with a messy mop of ginger hair, took offence. He grunted and pointed accusingly at the bloke in the other cell. 'I'm not a nonce,' he shouted at the top of his voice, still pointing at his mate who had pervy, shifty eyes, that darted from side to side. 'I'm a grass, but I've never been a nonce. He's a nonce, next door.'

We laughed and we laughed. There was a pecking order, even amongst the lowest type of prisoners. It was better to be a grass than a sex offender, even though being a grass was a pile of shit.

I had another laugh along the road at Parkhurst – I had been moved there again. Looking back, perhaps I shouldn't be laughing. It turned out that the vicar in Parkhurst was inviting all the weirdos, including the Yorkshire Ripper, to Bible readings and afternoon tea. Anyone who was sane never went. Sutcliffe was mad and went to Broadmoor, but he started his stretch at Parkhurst in 1981, where he was attacked by a Scottish prisoner called Jimmy Costello:

Jimmy followed Sutcliffe into the hospital wing at Parkhurst and cut him on the face with a broken coffee jar. The Ripper's wounds needed thirty stitches, and he didn't get any sympathy from anyone at all in the prison.

Apparently, the vicar refused to invite Graham Young, the teacup poisoner, to his little gatherings, for obvious reasons.

Young was a real oddball. He became fascinated by poisons when he was a young schoolboy and began to test them on relatives. He couldn't wait to see the poisons taking effect. They nicked him for trying to kill close family and a school friend. He went to Broadmoor to start with, and we were horrified when he arrived at Parkhurst. We knew he had tried to poison more than seventy people, and we kept him well away from the teapot.

It must say something that the vicar felt safer having people like the Yorkshire Ripper round for tea.

Neville the Devil was a real psycho. He was always washing his hands and his cell floor was like polished glass. Everywhere Neville went, the screws were a bit iffy: we knew he had the potential to cut people with a butcher's boning knife – he had more scars on his face than a map of the Underground. Even Reggie Kray warned us to be careful, because Neville turned on his own people. Reggie said Neville couldn't be trusted.

Neville and I got on really well, and he used to call me by my middle name, Luke. But I had to be careful. When he came into my cell, I lifted up my mattress and showed him a sharpened blade from a pair of garden shears. If ever I thought he was going to cut me I was ready to stab him. He ended up as one of my best friends, and we often sat down and had a bit of puff and all that. He had beautiful photos of his daughter and we used to look at them. When I did the money lending in jail, he would go around and make sure I got the interest back. We used to eat together, and had many chats about violence – but I kept that blade well sharpened.

Despite all this kind of excitement, one of the worst things about prison was the boredom. Charlie Richardson started organising what he called 'loon nights', where the weirdos told their stories. We had the nutters in, and they would tell us about their cases and their beliefs.

One night Charlie was in his cell with a couple of guys and he said, 'Tell Bobby what you just told me.'

This prisoner, called Jason turned to me and said, 'An angel came into my cell. It came down and it had big wings. It had bronze feet and fire coming out of its legs.'

I went, 'That is absolute bollocks. I'm not having that!'

His mate, Lennie the Lid, said, 'Yes, there was an angel. I saw it, too.'

I thought that was a real loony bin. I gave them a fiver to get a bit of puff and have more hallucinations. They were hanging around looking for a bit of puff anyway, and had hoped I would lend them the money, so I obliged.

Then there was a geezer called Fletcher. He had a scar down the side of his boat race where Ronnie Kray had cut him with a pin. Charlie called him in and asked him to tell me his tragic tale.

Fletcher had been a soldier, and had had a child with a woman who was messing about. He had this kid at his house sometimes, and one weekend she dropped the kid off.

Fletcher thought the world was so wicked that he didn't want the kid growing up in it. He strangled the kid, but then panicked because she was coming back to pick up her son. He cut a hole in the chair, broke a broom in half and stuck the handle up the kid's backside. So the kid was sitting there as if he was writing his homework, but he was as dead as a doornail. You can see the sort of nutters I was in with!

I met so many characters inside. There was Rocky, an ex-boxer who punched above his weight at Parkhurst. They nabbed him for armed robbery, and he was given seven years for his troubles.

Rocky was a six-foot, lean, mean fighting machine. He had short dark hair, a flat boxer's nose and dark brown eyes – quite a good-looking guy. Rocky was happy-go-lucky, enjoyed a laugh and everyone liked him. He also fancied himself as a bit of a chef.

Prisoners cooked their own meals because, that way, they knew what they were eating was safe. Prison officers worked in the kitchens, too, and did their best to supervise in there, checking on who had access to kitchen equipment. As it happened, everyone had blades hidden back in their cells anyway.

They kept the ingredients well away from people like the teacup poisoner. Parkhurst contained the country's most dangerous psychopaths and lunatics, so you can imagine how careful everyone was. Rocky always managed to find quality ingredients, and he cooked lovely meals for his mates.

This muscle man worked in the kitchens, which meant he was an early riser; the kitchen orderlies prepared breakfast and they worked while everyone else dozed in their cells. One morning, while he helped to prepare breakfast, Rocky assembled the ingredients he needed for the evening meal. His favourite dish was spag bol, and so he selected some mince, spaghetti, tomatoes and garlic (a speciality on the Isle of Wight), plus bacon, celery, carrots, onions, bay leaves, parmesan cheese and olive oil. I'm sure he put other stuff in it, but those were the main ingredients.

Rocky took what he could find in the kitchen and 'borrowed' ingredients from the other orderlies. As he checked his recipe against the stuff he'd got together, Rocky realised he was short of an onion. He spotted one in a cupboard, and added it to his food pile.

A nasty-sounding voice snapped: 'That's my fucking onion! You're a thief. Give me back my fucking onion.'

'Fuck off,' Rocky snarled, closing his bag of food with the onion well and truly buried in there.

He'd never liked Harry the Cook, a thug from the North who'd proved far too handy with swords and knives. He was a huge bloke, with an overhanging gut, string vest and smelly armpits. Despite that imposing frame, Rocky would have destroyed him in a bare-knuckle fight.

'That's my last onion, so I want it back now or you're going to get whacked.'

Rocky wasn't going to back down. 'You'll get it back some time – just fuck off. What would you want it for anyway? It would only make you cry, you big baby.'

'Give it back now, or you're brown bread.'

'Fuck off.'

Something was going to give as the battle for the onion became a verbal duel. In prison, you can never back down if you're challenged.

'I warned you,' Harry hissed as he reached behind one of the cupboards and produced a gleaming blade. He'd been using it under supervision while preparing the meals, but had hidden the kitchen knife instead of handing it back.

The sun flooded into the kitchen, with rays dancing around the shining pots and reflecting on Harry's razor-sharp knife. One thrust in the stomach and Rocky's blood was shooting out all over the place; Parkhurst had never seen so much claret spilled.

'Help me, help me,' Rocky pleaded, gasping for breath. Harry pushed the blade in as far as it would go and then removed it from my pal's bleeding stomach.

Alarm bells sounded all over the place and screws appeared from every corner of the prison. Rocky had lost too much blood; his face was a contorted mess as the pain surged through his body and, at the age of forty-one, he knew his time was up.

I was really upset. Rocky came from a lovely family and

was a solid guy and a dear friend to me; he also came from my manor, which made it even more personal. My heart went out to him and his family and I thought it was a waste of a good guy's life. He ended up dying because of an onion. I keep hearing people say that prison is a holiday camp; I don't know what holiday camps they go to, but they would shit their pants if they went to the ones frequented by the likes of Rocky and me.

Then there was a conman at Maidstone called Novak. He was a notorious type who used to do postal fraud. He was a Canadian Jew, and very well heeled – he was even connected with President Truman. He was a very wealthy man, a multi-millionaire. His daughter used to come in a Rolls-Royce to visit him.

An Indian kid called Pulak was running the laundry. We used to have our shirts starched and we wore tailored, made-to-measure clothes in prison. It was all bravado ... we used to smuggle in our own shoes and all that. This Pulak charged as much tobacco as he could for doing the work. He was a greedy bastard, but it ensured that Novak lived like a king.

Novak, a professional conman, used every trick in the book and you couldn't trust him. He was just a bit smarter than the rest. People threatened to bash him up, but his favourite reply to that was: 'I'm an old man with a weak heart.' He'd been arrested at the Dorchester Hotel while he was eating lobster thermidor. He used the 'old man, weak heart' line again and asked if they needed to embarrass him with handcuffs. He said he would go quietly, and so a copper walked him to the front door of the Dorchester. Suddenly, Novak span round and kicked the young copper in the bollocks. He then legged it up the road, bumped into another copper and was nicked.

After he told me that story he asked if I would become his minder, because so many people were chasing him. I was happy to look after him for money, because he was a character and made me laugh. When guys came looking for him after he'd pulled a stroke, I said, 'Fuck off. More mug you for falling for it.' He really conned Pulak, the young Indian kid, saying he had talent and would be useful in business later. Novak showed him pictures of flash cars and promised him the world. The conman could have anything he wanted, within reason, and it was all provided by Pulak.

Novak also had a scam where he used the girls in the prison office to type up letters as if from Harrods. The letters said that he was chief buyer there, and asked for free samples from overseas companies to see if they were good enough to sell in Harrods. So he had all this quality stuff coming in from abroad. He opened up a warehouse to keep it in, and then sold it to stall traders. He then said his operation had run into trouble, and couldn't pay the girls. They were furious, but what could they do? Instead, Novak offered them stock, which he said would be worth a lot more than their wages.

'You can have tights, because every woman wears tights,' he told them.

When the women went to sell the stuff they discovered that they were tights for pregnant women. Not quite what they expected.

Novak was even conning the screws as well, because they didn't believe he could con them. Everyone was bunging him and it just went on and on.

When he got out, the head of security was waiting because Novak was gate-arrested by the Royal Canadian Mounted Police as he left the prison. Apparently some of the conman's operations in Canada had been rumbled, so his freedom had lasted for only a few minutes.

As he left, he handed over an envelope to a screw, grassing on Pulak. It said: 'Bye. Don't be so greedy.'

Pulak was raided and all his tobacco was seized. Novak was a man who could not be trusted under any circumstances!

There was a big, fat geezer at Maidstone called Nagi who owned nightclubs and strip clubs in Wales. He was always talking about having anal sex with women. Nagi was a Pole and he was always eating. He had sandwiches everywhere, and he would eat anything. He asked me to get him stuff out of the kitchen. We managed to get him liver sausage and all that, and Nagi would buy it for double the usual price.

I was earning well off Nagi and he was my best customer. I paid the guy in the kitchen for giving me the stuff, but still made a good profit. Nagi was always buying food off people. If they were cooking a meal, he would say he wanted a bowl of it in exchange for a bit of tobacco. That guy just kept eating. He looked like Friar Tuck, and was just a glutton.

Nagi wasn't content with sausages and other meat, because one day he approached me: 'Bobby, I love a bit of rabbit. Could you get me some rabbit, please, so I can make a stew?'

Two Hell's Angels – lifers in the garden party – smuggled food in and out of the wing, so I asked them if they could get hold of a rabbit. They seemed willing, so I left them to it. I hadn't ordered a rabbit before, but felt confident that one would arrive to satisfy Nagi's enormous appetite.

Lo and behold, a couple of days later a parcel of grease-proof paper arrived on the wing with what looked like a fresh, skinned rabbit inside. *'Can't get much fresher than that,'* I thought, looking at the neatly packed animal.

'This looks just the job,' Nagi said. 'How much do I pay you for this rabbit?'

'A fiver will be a sweet deal,' I told him.

In those days we were getting a tiny allowance a week, so £5 was good money. This was good business. Anyway, he cooked the animal and ate it without any complaints.

I kept supplying him with this and that, including more sausages, some fresh fish, and the occasional rabbit. My scheme was working well, with Nagi paying on the dot and me rewarding the guy in the kitchen.

One day, Nagi ordered a collection of vegetables, nicked from the garden, and I knew what was coming.

'Bobby, I enjoyed those rabbits so much that I would like another one. Could you get me another rabbit?'

Outside, the garden party were happily digging away when they uncovered a gruesome sight – a pile of cat skins.

The screws assumed that the Hell's Angels had been performing some bizarre Satanic ceremony with the cats but, when word reached me, I feared that the cats had served a different purpose.

There were several cats around the prison, and they did a good job of keeping control of mice and rats. They lived in the boiler house in the winter, and that was where they had their kittens. We just called them the boiler house cats and left them to it.

I ran across the wing and confronted one of the Hell's Angels. 'What the fuck is going on? What's this about cats? Have you been selling me cats instead of rabbits?'

'It's the same thing,' one of them explained casually, not quite realising the gravity of the situation. 'With the head, tail and feet cut off, Nagi didn't notice the difference, did he?'

'That's not the fucking point,' I growled. 'I can't go and tell the geezer that I've been selling him cats instead of rabbits. Even worse, he's been eating them.'

I kept on supplying Nagi with all sorts of food, apart from rabbit. I explained that they had become scarce and difficult to get hold of. I tried to keep it all quiet, but stuff like that spreads like wildfire in prison. The guys all got stoned and couldn't keep their mouths shut. Everyone in the prison, except Nagi, knew that I had been providing him with cats to prepare his favourite stew.

The upshot was that whenever Nagi walked along the landing, everyone went: *'Meow, meow ...'*

Somehow he didn't twig but, on the day I was due to leave, I decided to come clean.

'Nagi, do you remember that I got you a couple of rabbits?'

'I had a couple of rabbits, yes,' Nagi recalled. 'Very nice they were, too, and succulent. They had quite a unique flavour and went very well with my carrots and onions. I used a traditional Polish recipe and should have given you a taste.'

'Nagi, I have to tell you that the –' I tried to say.

'Those rabbits were very, very nice.'

'Yes, but –' I tried again, still not able to get a word in edgeways.

'Are you saying that you could get me some more?' Nagi butted in, his voice growing louder with excitement.

'They were fucking *cats*,' I blurted out.

'What? What? Cats?'

'Nagi, I had no idea. They were sold to me as rabbits and that is the truth. Here's your money back.'

It didn't make much difference whether he believed me or not, and he wasn't interested in a refund. He stuck his fingers down his throat, even though the cats had been consumed a few months earlier, and reached for the slop bucket.

As I left my cell and prepared for the great outdoors, I could hear his words ringing in my ears: 'Bobby, you bastard … Bobby, you bastard! You fed me cats. You fed me fucking cats!'

'That stew must really have been the cat's whiskers,' I joked to myself as I left Nagi in his cell with an overflowing bucket.

There was another reason why prisoners liked to cook their own food and eat in their rooms: we risked our lives every time we went down to collect our meals. Usually we were in no hurry; it was best to avoid the queues as the mealtimes were really a madhouse.

At Parkhurst, I was on the middle floor with Charlie Richardson and Reggie Kray. We could look down and check on the length of the queue. After the cells opened in the morning, a member of Charlie's firm would bring up hot water for our tea. Charlie had a big, square table in his cell, so we usually sat around that for a cuppa and a chat.

One breakfast time, an Irishman called Francis McGee was queuing, innocent as you like, when another inmate, John Paton, produced a blade and stabbed McGee to death. It was all in the papers. What was Paton doing in there? They must have known he'd killed another prisoner in Wakefield with a bed leg in a row over home-made booze. In Parkhurst, that was a killing just waiting to happen.

This time, Paton had filed down a piece of steel and stabbed McGee nine times. Amazingly, the row was about a game of chess. McGee admitted cheating in a game of chess years previously and made a joke about it. Paton didn't think it was funny, so he went back to his cell, collected his weapon and that was the end of McGee. Alarm bells went off and screws were running everywhere.

The killer of Muriel McKay, Nizamodeen Hosein, cradled McGee's head in his arms. I might be cynical – that's what prison does to you – but I couldn't help but wonder whether

'Nez' was looking for a good report and early parole. Hosein had some history: he and his brother had tried to kidnap the wife of Rupert Murdoch and had mistakenly made off with the wife of Murdoch's deputy chairman instead. Hosein and his brother didn't get the £1 million ransom money they wanted, so they executed Muriel and fed her to pigs on a Hertfordshire farm.

As Hosein held McGee in his arms and screws tried desperately to stop the flow of blood, Fred – a lifer who'd been reckless with a shooter – inched his podgy frame along the landing, and he stopped to chat to Charlie and me as he went past. We knew Fred well; he always just concentrated on his own problems.

'He's taking a fucking liberty there,' said Fred. 'Taking a fucking liberty.'

We agreed. 'Yeah, you're right. It's a fucking madhouse in here.'

'Taking a fucking liberty,' Fred went on. 'There's blood all over my cornflakes.'

'You what?' Charlie turned around in disbelief. 'For fuck's sake, there's a geezer dying down there.'

'Not my problem. Look, there's blood in my cornflakes.'

'Well, if you're so worried, you can have mine,' Charlie offered. 'Can't be bothered with breakfast after seeing that.'

Pandemonium continued downstairs, and we were ushered into our cells.

Half an hour later we were unlocked again and Fred appeared at Charlie's cell door. 'Is it still OK to take your cornflakes, Charlie?' He hadn't forgotten the offer from one of England's most notorious criminals.

Back at Maidstone, Herbie the hippy brought in opium. His drug connections got him inside in the first place. There was more gear in that nick than there was outside. Everyone was tripping every weekend. They were all out of their nuts. If they weren't tripping, they were all pissed up in the cells. As long as there was no aggravation, the screws didn't worry.

I remember at Maidstone being friendly with one guy who was doing bird for killing his wife. Most murderers were in for killing their wives. This man's old woman had been a prostitute. He was a lovely man, a gentle soul who'd gone out to work every day and all that. But she was having it away with every Tom, Dick and Harry. When he came home one night he pulled her about it, and accused her of going with different men; the information had come from the neighbours. Then, after he was in bed, he jumped up, stabbed her, and chopped her up into little bits.

To get rid of the evidence, he started to take her out in his lunchbox and bury parts of her all over the place. And when, finally, the police knocked on his door because people hadn't seen her, he admitted that he'd killed her. The young copper who was interviewing him asked where the body was. Well, he took them to a place, lifted up a stone and pulled her head out. The copper who was handcuffed to him fainted. But he got manslaughter when they heard about all she'd done and all the provocation.

There was a cell thief at Maidstone who nicked stuff and left notes signed 'Robin Hood'. One day, Robin Hood went into Bobby Abbs's cell and stole his tobacco. Bobby had been nicked on drugs charges, but on this occasion he was concerned about the loss of his legal substance. The note left said: 'Ta mate, Robin Hood.'

Bobby Abbs came out onto the landing and yelled, 'He's nicked a quarter ounce of my tobacco. Robin Hood's been here.'

'Well, you can't catch him,' I said. 'He's done and dusted and he's gone. Just keep your cell shut in future.'

So Bobby went to go for a shower. His family made sure he received the best toiletries from home. He looked for his bar of soap – Imperial Leather with that distinctive red wrapper – but only the wrapper remained. Robin Hood had nicked the soap as well.

Then there was a guy called Woodbine Willie. He and a bloke called Johnnie the Aussie were a right pair of oddballs. They'd made a safe in a locker, all out of solid wood, and hid their stuff in there for Christmas.

But Robin Hood found out that the safe had a plywood back. So he ripped the back off and nicked all their goodies. This sort of thing would be talked about for weeks, we were so starved of anything interesting to think or talk about.

Also at Maidstone there was Dukey Osborne, who was a friend of the Krays. He used to stand on the landing on reception day, watching the new geezers coming in. He used to go, 'Coo coo, little chickens, little chickens.'

He always had his shorts on and he would invite the kids up to his cell, get them stoned, and the next thing they would come out with sore arses. He never tried it on with any of us lot, but he got all those kids who came from the sticks; it was like Christmas for Dukey.

During visiting time, after all the searches, we would talk about the same old things with the people who came to see us. We could catch up on family events, and check on the health of aunts and uncles.

We would also spy in the visiting room, because you could always pick out the wife or girlfriend who was on the brink of leaving her man. For a start, they would gaze around the room, instead of looking at the geezer who was being visited. Also, those women were always the first to leave the room.

Of course, we knew who the prisoner was and could tell that he would be receiving a 'Dear John' letter saying it was all over. Then we would see the bloke in tears, reading the heartbreaking note from the wife or girlfriend.

There was a guy called Frank – yet another Frank – in Parkhurst who preyed on the victims of failed romances. He wore a headband, and looked like an Apache. He had a dark complexion, but it was no tan; it was grime. He hadn't washed for five years. We called him Dirty McSquirty and he smelled so badly that we suggested that he should have his own wing of the prison. He was a strange character who dyed his hair with black shoe polish.

Anyway, he'd perfected his message to rejected, virtually suicidal prisoners: 'Your woman has just left you, but there is a bright side. You've still got your wedding ring, and we can trade it in for some gear. You won't want to wear the ring, as it will only bring back memories.'

After Frank's stunt, I usually stepped in. As I was the prison 'banker', I offered cash for the ring, and then Frank would seek out the local drugs dealer. He would buy some puff and take it back to the heartbroken prisoner's cell. Frank and the miserable prisoner would then get stoned and try and work out why their hopeless lives had disintegrated.

Frank had a budgie called Boy Boy and the bird used to fly up and down the landing, performing tricks before flying back to a beautiful cage. Boy Boy was 'doing his bird' too, I suppose.

One time, some of the guys ran out of puff and needed to get some money. They sent Frank out to see if he could fix a deal with the IRA, as they usually had some drugs. But when Frank was gone, they wrung Boy Boy's neck.

They laid Boy Boy on the bed and, when Frank got back, they told him: 'Frank, something terrible has happened. Boy Boy got caught in the door when it shut and he's dead. We're so, so sorry, Frank.'

With Frank in tears, they suggested: 'There is one good thing. We could sell the cage to get a bit of puff!'

Frank went along with the plan to sell the cage as he needed some puff, too. That's what it was like in there.

Frank had a point, though: continuing a relationship with a long-term prisoner is pointless. At Maidstone prison

I came across a fellow called Richard. Richard was a lovely guy. He was a 'happy hippy' and had been done for drugs. Because of that he was disowned by his family.

Richard's wife wrote to him all through his sentence; he went down for seven years or so. He was making plans for when he got out; the two of them were going to sail off into the sunset and all that.

A week before Richard was released, his wife told him she'd been living with a guy for three years. Her intentions were honourable. She'd thought that if she stuck by him it would get Paul through his sentence. That night he got his bit of puff, went into his cell and hanged himself.

All the prisoners felt really guilty because we didn't know what had happened. At first, we thought it was something one of us had said. Richard's death caused a ripple effect through the wing. You could feel the atmosphere. It was really bad. We had a church service for him and they played 'Starry Starry Night' and all that. A guy played it on the guitar.

That's why, when you go to jail for a long sentence, the first thing you have to do is get rid of your wife or girlfriend. You have to dump them, because you can't lie in bed at night, driving yourself mad, wondering who she's shagging or whatever she's doing. You just crack up.

It's best that they have their freedom, and you can get your head around surviving the sentence. After all, she didn't commit any crime. It's not normal for women to spend all that time with the kids on their own. People have needs, and most women definitely have physical needs.

When I heard women come up to their guy and say, 'I'll wait for you,' I always thought it was a load of bollocks. You have to be kind to the person you're leaving behind. As I said, if you are a gentleman, you will end the relationship there and then. That's what I did, and it worked for me and my then partner. The ones who will stick by you are your family such as brothers, sisters, mums and dads. If you've got a bird and you're looking at a long sentence, park her up, otherwise you'll go stir crazy. If you get out and your wife is still about and you are still in love, then you can start again.

Soon after Richard's death, another prisoner hanged himself – probably because of all those thoughts in his head. He was found hanging in his cell. The screws went off to get a body bag and the idiots left his cell door open. When they came back, his radio had gone, his bedding had gone and his tobacco had disappeared. The vultures had been in. The trainers on his feet had been taken off while he was still hanging; they even took his trousers, so he was hanging there in his underpants. They took the fucking lot! Bless his heart, he was taken away in the body bag and disposed of.

I often hear people say prison is like Butlin's. Well, I think Butlin's should sue. That's what the public don't see: the heartache, the crime and the violence in prison. The public think that everything is all right because someone is locked up and there will be no more trouble. Crime doesn't stop in prison.

No one would have shed a tear if the Yorkshire Ripper had topped himself. In fact, everyone would have cheered. And I'm sure no one is waiting for him on the outside.

CHAPTER TWELVE
A SOLITARY VOICE

I've always loved poetry, and decided to put my thoughts down in verse. Much of my inspiration came when I was in solitary confinement.

They were still moving me from prison to prison and back again because that's what they did with dangerous, subversive people like me. On one occasion, I was ghosted from Albany to Bristol prison, where I was in total lockdown. They gave me that treatment after the incident with the governor. It meant I was isolated from all other prisoners; when they opened my door for exercise, the prison was locked down. I used to exercise mostly at night, walking around a yard on my own with prison officers on each corner and two dog handlers patrolling me. No one spoke.

Total lockdown was seen as an extreme punishment, but I loved it. I could read all the books I wanted, and didn't have to listen to all the usual bollocks going on in the main prison.

I had started writing poems at Albany and continued at Bristol, Maidstone and Parkhurst. I drew inspiration from many sources. One day I was in solitary, enjoying a book by

Tom Sharpe called *Riotous Assembly*. It was a send-up of South Africa's apartheid system. The book was so funny that I rolled around the bed, laughing, tears rolling down my cheeks.

The principal prison officer and two of his bully boys opened up the cell and said, 'Are you on fucking drugs or what? You're in solitary – what have you got to laugh about?'

'He's fucking mad, this one,' one of the other guards hissed. 'He takes hostages and causes sit-downs and riots. We need to keep a close eye on this bastard.'

My reputation was well deserved. Apart from the 'hostage' drama with the governor, I organised a massive sit-in all over the country from my cell in Maidstone. It was over conditions such as visiting and food.

Then there was the Albany riot of 1983 when they wrecked the place, set fire to wings and all that. More than twenty prisoners were charged with mutiny and did more bird to draw attention to their poor conditions. I'd actually been helping to plan the riot before I took the governor hostage. I was moved away after that, but would have taken part if I'd been there.

I was still laughing as I continued reading my book, and the poems just flowed. I had to write them with a pencil on sheets of toilet paper. Then I smuggled them from the solitary confinement block in the wrappers of Mars Bars and Crunchies. I slipped the wrapped-up poems between the cheeks of my arse, so that when they rubbed me down for a body search they didn't find anything.

I would return to the main prison, after my stints in solitary, and write my previous works down on real paper. I still have those poems today. When I read them now, my mind travels back to every incident, exactly as it happened.

I've always been inspired by Kipling's poem, 'If'. He wrote it in 1895, but the work is as relevant today as it ever was. You could say that I kept my head when all about me lost theirs and blamed everything on me. I trusted myself when all men doubted me. I made allowances for their doubting. I was lied about and hated. But I didn't deal in lies and I had a dream. I endured years of nightmares until that dream came true.

The vicar came to my cell in Bristol and he went: 'How on earth can you stand this total isolation? I couldn't do it.'

'Don't you like yourself, vicar?' I asked him. 'I like me. I like my company. Also, I can read all I want, and I have a nice, warm heating pipe here that keeps me snug. Your establishment has played all its cards, but I haven't even begun to play mine yet. I ain't broken.'

My message to the authorities was, 'So you are all fucked. What can you do now? Put me in prison? I'm already in prison. You have nothing else to threaten me with. It's not what you can do to me any more – it's what I can do to you.'

THE ONE WHO LOCKED MY DOOR

I have seen dark souls within these walls
Each man's sins made the cross he bore
Yet no darker soul did I ever see
Than the one that locked my door

I have seen men's souls cry out in pain
I have seen men beaten to the floor
I have seen men stripped and abused
By the one who locked my door

I have been to the place they put us men
Who refuse to bow and crawl
Our honour is written in the red of blood
Written on those four walls

There is no level they will not stoop
They torture men night and day
I have watched them abuse the food we eat
And beat men whilst they pray

I have seen the chaplain give sacrament
To men beaten beyond repair
Kneel down and pray to our Lord
And pretend the blood was not there

But our dear Lord was one of us
And he will keep the score
And he will judge those blackest souls
The ones who locked my door.

The vicar was totally gobsmacked. He deserves his star-
ring role in 'The one who locked my door'. But I wasn't being
rude to a nice guy – he knew about the violence that was

meted out to prisoners and turned a blind eye to it; he just carried on with his religious business as usual. I was never beaten up, just kept away from everyone. I thought that if ever there was a complete hypocrite, that guy fitted the bill.

That experience made me wary of vicars and anyone religious, but I became interested in Buddhism. One regular visitor, a lovely Buddhist monk, Anju, is one of my best friends today. He followed me from prison to prison to teach me Buddhism. He used to come in and I would say, 'Hello, skinhead.' I really loved the guy. He was the gentlest person I ever met. He would say, 'Don't let them get under your skin. Don't get angry with them. Just look at them as colours of blue. That way they can't wind you up.'

I was a volatile person, hating everyone, but the monk helped me control my anger. He opened up my mind to get beyond that anger.

Anju went on to become spiritual adviser to the King of Thailand. He was also awarded an OBE. That made me smile, because to a Buddhist it meant nothing! They aren't into accolades or anything like that. Prison showed me brutality; Anju showed me humanity.

Lynn, the prison librarian at Maidstone, was fascinated by my poems, especially 'The one who locked my door'.

'This is deep stuff,' she said. 'Where did you write this?'

'That was written in solitary in Albany. That was when they were kicking people to pieces in there.'

'You should have your poems published,' she told me, reading through some of my other work.

I made some enquires and talked to Tony Benn, the government minister, who was in contact with me all the time I was inside. Later on, he was to champion all of my campaigns to educate and rehabilitate prisoners. He wrote a foreword to have the book published, but the prison took it away and wouldn't let me take the project any further.

Lynn and I became very good friends because of those poems. Later, on home leave, we became romantically involved.

Those poems came straight from the heart and reflected my circumstances at the time. When I wrote them I was an angry young man with no hope, but I did eventually see the light and make a dramatic turnaround.

CHAPTER THIRTEEN
THE UNIVERSITY
OF CRIME

Prison had a horrendous effect on my mum. With my dad dead, and members of her family in prison, she was heartbroken. She never visited me, Freddy or Frankie. I kept in touch with my brothers, but I didn't see them as I had to be kept in much more secure units. Mum wrote to me, and I sent her plenty of letters. My sisters used to visit me regularly, but my mum found it too difficult to go near the prison gates.

The university of crime is a place where villains teach other villains everything they know. If a kid goes to college, he or she learns up to a certain level. If they go to university, that level increases. If they win a place at Oxford or Cambridge, the standard increases even more. It's very similar in the prison system; the only difference is that, in jail, the main subject is crime.

If you send young people into maximum-security prisons they will meet terrorists, drug smugglers, top fraudsters, arms dealers and all sorts of people. I met the American Mafia, Tong, Triads, the IRA, the UDA, people who specialised in forged documents, cartels and all that. When you are in there you are living together 24/7, like you do at university, so of course people learn from each other.

You are learning, talking to each other, and you come out with a degree in organised crime. You know how terrorists make bombs; how drugs smugglers evade customs; how to create false identities; where to buy guns, what sort of guns to buy; and how to carry out more efficient armed robberies.

We had prisoners from foreign countries in there. One time, a group of them asked how many police we had in Britain. Someone told them, and then they asked how many villains there were.

'And you do what they tell you? Why don't you just shoot them?' they told us.

That was the mentality of foreign criminals. They were filling our heads with all that.

It's a violent, dark world and – as I keep stressing – there's no glamour in it. You get people coming out addicted to drugs when they've never used drugs before. Some kids think it's glamorous to mix with gangsters, but they get eaten alive in jail.

You have to have a reputation before you go in, and belong to a firm, or else you become known as a Hobbit – you know, those dopey-looking things that would look out of place at any university.

There were nights when you would go and eat with the IRA. They talked about bombs and incendiary devices. They wanted to disrupt the prisons at the time, and cause strikes and all that. We all got involved in those. The IRA had a political agenda; they weren't criminals like us. They would manipulate criminals to create sit-downs and riots in prisons.

When I met the Tong, they were usually inside for dealing in millions of pounds' worth of heroin. In prison all the Chinese stuck together, but I got to know one of the top men, who was called Sheng.

One day, he said, 'Brother, come and eat with us. When you come out of here, brother, you come and see me. We will make you good money.'

Sheng saw me as 'good stuff'. I was violent in those days – I'd had a few fights in prison, and he knew I was a bit lively.

Well, I liked Chinese food so I went to eat with them. I used to sit with him and he was waited on hand and foot by all his underlings.

He said people had grassed on them and he wanted the grasses sorted out. He didn't like 'Chinese doing Chinese', and wanted me to do a bit of work. He also told me how much money there was in the heroin game, but I told him that wasn't my style. I said I was an armed robber and that was what I did.

'But guns are guns. You shoot people. If you shoot people for me, I will pay you big money.'

I politely declined his offer.

Then there was the American Mafia. A group of them were arrested in England when they landed to change planes after a $15 million bond swindle. They were arrested with all those bent bonds and they got ten years each. At Maidstone, I got on really well with them – Jimmy, Charlie and a couple of others. They'd ask me to get some meatballs nicked from the kitchen because they wanted to make spag bol.

'Come to see us in America when we get out of here,' Jimmy would say. 'You're a good boy, Bobby.'

They didn't know how the British jail system worked, so I told them all about it. In return, they told me about the rackets that went down in America, including the way they carried out frauds and extortion rackets.

You could tell they were the Mafia because they had a certain way about them. They lived well and had everything they wanted. Jimmy thought he was a bit of an artist, although he wasn't very good. He painted teeth pure white, like in the toothpaste adverts, and it all looked a bit false. Jimmy was highly educated, and Charlie was a minder – a really heavy bit of work.

They told me how I could do better armed robberies. They said I was too near the front; they said I had to sit back and let the soldiers do the work. I learned more about the structure of organised crime from people like the Mafia and the Triads, something that had really helped me when I got out after my manslaughter sentence and organised all the armed robberies.

It's crazy to put young offenders into a situation where they are meeting terrorists and people like that. Because prisons are too full, people who shouldn't be in together have to be, and they are learning from each other. For example, I can teach you how to be a subversive – I learned all that off the IRA. (You go in, rip the plumbing out and flood the prison. Where do you put the prisoners then?)

All we hear nowadays is hard talk about taking away this privilege and that privilege. But if this prison or that prison goes up in smoke during a riot, look at the amount of money it will take to replace the jail! Prisoners are at risk because old scores get settled in a riot and guys stab each other. Prison officers get injured, too.

Overcrowding means members of the public are more at risk. If prisoners escape, then members of the public are injured. Guys who escape know that the next time they will receive a life sentence, but they don't give a shit. If you get in their way they're going to hurt you, because they're not planning to get caught and start that life sentence.

We need a proper rehabilitation programme. Some minor crimes don't need prison sentences. People should be sent to training centres and rehabilitation places, and that would be their sentence. They would attend a full course of training. These people need to be put back into work in the construction industry, trades like plumbing or even green industries. We should be training them to cope with the twenty-first century, not the eighteenth century.

Britain has also got to get rid of this 'three strikes and you're out' system that was imported from America. In the old days, if a burglar was a non-violent offender he got a lower sentence. Now if you are a burglar and you have three offences, you are going to get a really long sentence. So, if you are faced with that long sentence and you are non-violent, you could decide not to leave any witnesses behind after your next robbery. Now you have a potentially violent person who received no credit for his non-violent crimes.

After the Great Train Robbery, sentences became ridiculous. The gang captured the public's imagination, and made the authorities look foolish, so the government declared war on armed robbers. Sentences tripled. Before, if you were an armed robber, ten years was a big sentence. When they sentenced people to thirty and forty years, armed robbers decided they might as well shoot the people while doing the bit of work and leave no witnesses behind. That was being said to us in the university of crime.

This university for criminals also taught me some lethal ways of hurting people. You learned how to adapt and make weapons – when you were released you were fully versed in the subject. You also learned how to conceal them, as you had to get past the prison officers during the searches; the drug smugglers taught us how to do that.

A prisoner could develop a lethal list of weapons from everyday goods. If we had a plastic toothbrush, we warmed up the plastic and got one of those disposable razors with twin blades. We put the two blades in it to create a cut-throat weapon.

You could also get a six-inch nail from one of the work-shops, hammer it into shape and that became a stiletto. The

IRA did that, then soaked a nail in shit and stabbed the prison governor. They nearly killed him because he developed toxaemia.

Another way of doing someone was to get a couple of light bulbs, grind them up and add the tiny fragments to sugar. That had to be one of the worst punishments, with the glass fragments cutting away inside the body.

You could also put billiard balls or batteries in socks to cosh people with. Another trick was to run a razor through garlic. When you cut someone's arse with it the skin puffed up, it was more difficult to stitch, and they were left with a nasty scar.

Horrible, horrible stuff – but all part of the learning process.

I learned a lot about how to be a better villain in the university of crime. I finally decided, though, that I had no use for that information personally. Instead, I used the university of crime to get a proper education – and that was all down to Charlie Richardson.

It started off with Charlie at Parkhurst. Charlie and I got on very well. He loved books, and he had this thing about getting educated. He used to read books all the time in his cell. He would say to me, 'Bobby, read these books. Good boy, good boy.'

The books would be about mineralogy, politics, philosophy, business or the stock exchange. He used to have press cuttings about minerals and what was going up and down in the marketplace. Charlie was years ahead of his time, and he went out to South Africa to buy mining rights. Everyone else was thinking local while he was thinking global.

He said that I was different to a lot of the morons doing bird because I actually had a brain.

Charlie was so switched on. He was too intelligent to be in jail. You could spend the night with him and it would be fascinating. Charlie would feed into your ambition and motivate you. He was family to me and was always there for me. He was a small pawn, caught up in a big political game: he had bugged Harold Wilson's office. It was in the mid-1960s, and the South African intelligence services believed Wilson was a communist and might have sympathies with their opponents. Charlie told me that a cleaning firm bugged Wilson's office and it was a really easy job to organise. He simply put the right people in touch with each other.

He went on about the importance of being educated, and it rubbed off on me. If you talked to Reggie Kray, he'd be looking at a map of North London and saying, 'I could have this when I get out, or that area ...' I thought to myself that I'd already had all of that; I also knew that the manors were full of teenagers who would blow people's heads off because they were stoned and didn't give a shit.

And Charlie reminded me that if I went out armed robbing again, I would end up doing life inside or I would be shot dead. I wasn't keen on either of his options. He gave me the third alternative, and I preferred that.

'You have to take the other route,' Charlie said to me one day, his intense blue eyes penetrating my very soul as he held a batch of books aloft. 'You have to go down the road of education. You will get respect, you will be writing your own cheques, and you won't get shot.'

While I was at Parkhurst, some of the country's most dangerous men were writing letters, having debates with the governor about prison rules, and gaining qualifications. I have to say that Charlie started it all off, and I followed his example, later, of getting prisoners to use their brains. Some of those debates would have made a trained barrister proud. I'm sure that the prison authorities would have preferred BBC radio and the Open University to be outlawed as subversive organisations. Screws were trained to deal with dangerous prisoners, not to watch them taking part in debates or organise classes for newly educated inmates.

BBC Radio 4 and the Open University taught prisoners to behave like decent human beings. The prisons normally dealt with moronic thugs who were used to the language of violence. I'm sure that the authorities saw educated prisoners as the ones who might cause trouble; we could write to MPs, newspapers and even the Home Secretary. We thought nothing of writing informed letters to the Chief Inspector of Prisons. Imagine a governor's horror when the inspector replied to our letters and came for a look around!

Prisoners who listened to debates on the radio and embarked on Open University courses were viewed with great suspicion. Later on, when I looked at prison budgets, I was amazed to see the amount spent on security, which only turned out brutalised, angry men who would offend again. Charlie and I campaigned to have more spent on therapy and education to turn out humane and safe prisoners.

No matter what you talked to Charlie about, he knew the subject off by heart. You have to remember he was inside for a very long time. Charlie was a sponge for knowledge. No doubt about it: if he'd been born into a middle-class background he would have ended up in the House of Lords as one of the top goers.

As Charlie shook the books above his head to emphasise his point, then dropped them on the table for extra effect, I knew that my life was about to change for ever.

'You need to get out of here and into the Open University at Maidstone. They do a good job there. Get on with it.'

When Charlie spoke forcefully, you didn't argue. I knew he had my best interests at heart, and I mulled over what he said. Luckily, I knew a good prison officer at Parkhurst – they're not all bad – and we got on well. He was called Foxy, and I believe Charlie had a word with him. Foxy put forward my case for going to Maidstone, although it wasn't going to be easy because I'd caused chaos there during a previous stay.

I knew from Charlie that if I went down the learning route then I would lose out on money. In my day, if you worked in the tailor's shop or the kitchen, you were paid top money. If you went into education, to better yourself, the money didn't add up to much. So everyone who wanted to buy extra goodies went into sweatshops, not thinking of the future.

Off I went to Maidstone, then, wondering about my reception committee. After all, I'd been thrown out of the place a few years earlier for organising strikes, sit-downs and all that.

As soon as I walked through the door – heavily escorted – I spotted the deputy governor. I remembered that I'd thrown a bucket of shit over him.

He came over to me and said, 'Any sort of riot or anything like that, and I'll have you moved again.'

'Well, you moved me last time and I'm back again,' I answered, with a few swear words thrown in.

The deputy governor and his staff knew that I was well connected. I received letters from Lord Longford, Tony Benn, the Duke of Devonshire and other big players. The deputy governor was a bit wary of me. He had been on the wrong end of the riots at Durham jail, and I doubted he would rise to be governor.

Anyway, I went to see the governor himself, Colin Allan, and he asked me, 'If I give you a job in the education department, would you work there?'

'Yes,' I said, 'because it would give me access to books, education programmes and all that. I'll go on condition that you back me for an Open University degree.'

'Well, I'll put a word in for you and see what can be done.'

'Otherwise, fuck the lot of you,' I muttered. 'I'll just sit in my cell. I'm living all right.'

Looking back, with my record, and the things I said, I consider myself fortunate to be given such a chance.

To be fair to the governor, he did then come to see me and said I could have a job in the education department. I knew they wanted me off the wing anyway, in case I wound up the other prisoners and started more riots. Plus, I was well into my prison sentence. And, being a recognised troublemaker, sweatshops were never an option.

So, I went into the education block and started my learning process, studying sociology, psychology and all that. The Open University was brilliant, all the way through.

My job – education orderly – meant that I could read all the books I wanted and concentrate on my studies. Maidstone prison at the time was a training prison. Mr Allan was a decent man who cared about prisoners and encouraged education and rehabilitation, backing my ideas to the hilt.

I'd describe him as 'enlightened'. When my mum was ill with cancer, I had had to go to see her with three sets of handcuffs on and a chain that went down my leg. I was also handcuffed to a screw. Mum had wanted to stay at home instead of going into hospital: when I visited, there were armed police all around her flat. Nearer to the end of my sentence, Mr Allan was good enough to let me visit my mother before she died, without the handcuffs on – even though everyone told him that I would escape.

Before I went, he called me into his office and told me if I gave him my word he would let me go home without cuffs. He said I would be supervised by the chief education officer,

Major Bev Bingham. Major Bingham and the senior probation officer at Maidstone were really the ones who showed
me humanity there.

'Do you regret having me?' I asked my mum as she lay in
her bed, close to death.

'I don't regret anything, Bobby,' she told me. 'The only
regret I have is that you robbed the Bank of Ireland. That's
where I bank, and I have to see the manager all the time!'

I knew that my life of crime had actually broken her
heart, but she kept her humour as she approached the end
of her life. I told her about my education, the Open University
and everything, and it brought a smile to her face. She said
I had seen the light.

The governor had understood how a prisoner's mind
worked and had studied the rules of the organised criminals. He knew that by my giving him my word, those were
the strongest handcuffs he could put me in. The hierarchy
had put their jobs on the line for me; I appreciated that and
the visit went off without incident. Mind you, playing it
straight did me no favours with the screws: it seemed that
they had been taking bets on me absconding, and my good
behaviour cost them a lot of money.

My cell was searched on a regular basis for a month after
that. I was standing on the landing during one of these
occasions, talking to my pal, Joe Mooney, when a screw
came up to me.

'Got a minute?' he asked, without emotion.

'What do you want?' I barked back.

'Just to tell you that your mum is dead,' he said, looking for a reaction.

'Thanks a lot. Now fuck off.'

I was ripped apart inside, but in those places you can't show any sign of weakness. I waited until I was alone in my cell, held my head in my hands and mourned my mother.

Major Bingham showed genuine sympathy after my mum's death, and he was keen to push for my education. When I applied to do the Open University degree, he and Maurice, the probation officer, spoke up for me.

The governor let me go full steam ahead for my degree.

This was a whole new ball game for me, as nobody in my family had gone to university. That way of life was for posh kids, but here I was – a 'fresher' – giving my all to the Open University, and enjoying every minute.

It gave me such a real good feeling inside and I threw myself into the studies. I expected the tutors to be snobs and treat us like second-rate people, but they didn't; they gave us all the support we needed and went more than the extra mile.

The screws, on the other hand, would try to put a spanner in the works by sending our assignments in late. Many of the screws didn't have an O-level between them, and they didn't like the thought of us becoming qualified. The tutors were wise to that trick and gave us some leeway.

I became more and more engrossed in sociology and psychology. I remember one day reading a book about social deviants and thinking, 'That's me!' I knew I was different to most people, but now I could put a name to it. This was interesting stuff; I was reading about what made people like me tick. It wasn't just about getting a degree; it was about understanding my mind and finding the tools to turn my life around.

I decided to be an example of what could be achieved. I saw my future in front of me.

I was definitely going straight.

I sat in my cell and thought about the wise words of Charlie Richardson. It was a 'eureka' moment for me. Everything fell into place after reading that book. If I had all this education, what was the point in slipping back into crime? I paced around my small cell and punched the air. *'Fuck the past,'* I thought. *'Bring on my future.'*

I wasn't worried about leaving my mates behind in this new world; I worked out ways of taking them with me. If anyone thought I was going soft, then that was their problem – there was even a rumour going round that I was being nicer to the screws! I knew that changing my entire life around would be the hardest task I had ever set myself.

I began to spread the message that the government spent millions of pounds of taxpayers' money sending people through the revolving doors of prison. I could see that, if they trained more prisoners for employment and pushed Open University courses, it would save the country a fortune.

I was constantly highlighting the importance of educating prisoners. In most prisons, education wasn't encouraged by the screws and above: the last thing they wanted was educated prisoners organising petitions and all that. Charlie Richardson had been a right thorn in their side with his campaigns and protests, and I was following his example.

You have no idea what it felt like to receive a certificate in prison for qualifying with a Higher National Diploma in architecture, law and a mix of courses. After prison, I kept going at the University of Greenwich and was awarded my Open University degree there.

The Open University concept dates back to the autumn of 1962, when the idea of external degrees for London University was suggested. At the same time, the Ministry of Education and the BBC were talking about a 'college of the air', while the Labour Party debated the problems of lower-income groups entering higher education. Again, the idea was to launch a 'university of the air' on radio and television.

In stepped Harold Wilson, fresh from his 1964 election success, with enthusiasm for the project. He appointed Jennie Lee as Minister for the Arts and asked her to move the scheme forward.

She was the one who blew a hole in the wall of hostility and indifference facing any future for alternative university plans. I also had to climb that wall while I was in prison.

Such a massive project couldn't be established overnight. By 1967 Harold Wilson's cabinet had set up a planning committee to work towards an Open University. In 1969 the first vice-chancellor was appointed. In September of that year the newly born organisation was working feverishly in the new town of Milton Keynes, with a staff of just over seventy.

In 1971 the Open University welcomed its first students. These 25,000 determined souls were about to study subjects including the arts, social sciences and maths. And they did not need prior qualifications to reap the benefits.

Jennie Lee, who continued to back the Open University and became its first founder, said: 'I knew it had to be a university with no concessions, right from the very beginning. After all, I have gone through the mill myself, taking my own degree, even though it was a long time ago. I knew all about the conservatism and vested interests of the academic world. I didn't believe we could get it through if we lowered our standards.'

I can confirm that those standards have remained high since I turned my back on crime and concentrated on my education.

CHAPTER FOURTEEN

UNLOCKING THE FUTURE

My friends and family staged the party to beat all parties just before I was released for the final time in 1988. I went on a weekend of home leave and was stunned to find that the Prince of Wales pub in Holloway Road had been transformed for the occasion.

There was even a huge cake, adorned with sweet models of handcuffs and a sawn-off shotgun.

Everyone was buying drinks for me. There were so many drinks that I had to pour most of them down the sink. I didn't want to get pissed, knowing I had to behave and return to jail. Also, with so much time in solitary, I wasn't used to too much alcohol.

It was like a party for a dad coming home from the war. My schoolboy friends were there: Tony the Greek, Andy the Greek and Chrissy, to name but a few. The Major who'd patched us up all those years ago appeared as well, but he only stayed for an hour or so. He was paranoid when he saw loads of police outside. They were taking pictures of the well-known faces walking in the door, no doubt hoping to nick someone they were looking for. As revenge, I told one of the boys to get a camera and he started to take pictures of the Old Bill!

It was all getting a bit much for me, so I phoned up my girlfriend Lynn and asked if she would come to the party. She agreed, coming over all the way from her home in Kent, and was flabbergasted when she saw the scene before her.

'This is crazy,' she gasped, as drinks were poured and people came up to me, handing over 'respect' money to give me a good start. 'I've never seen anything like this before.'

Every time Lynn had a drink, another ten appeared beside her. She stayed by my side during that weekend and that gave me such a good feeling. She knew that people were assuming I would be back robbing banks. Despite offer after offer, that was never an option. I had decided to go straight.

The feeling of joy when you're released from prison is difficult to explain. The shackles are off as you enter a new world, and you believe you are ready to start afresh. But the entire planet is against you as soon as loyal companions wave goodbye and the prison gates open.

That first day of freedom, leaving the prison gates at Maidstone on a bright, sunny day in 1988, seemed like a momentous event at the beginning of my new life. A hired Rolls-Royce picked me up and Lynn and I had a whale of a time at another homecoming party. It was a follow-up to the Prince of Wales do, and was the beano to beat all beanos.

When I came out of prison and decided to go straight, things didn't always go my way. Sceptics wondered when I would be back in prison. I had to remember that I lived in this society and needed to obey the rules.

Ultimately, it's about your choice and commitment in leaving it all behind. Some people have a stronger commitment than others. Some people have better chances than others – I am lucky because, when I was in prison, I managed to educate myself. I came out and followed an academic career. I did have to start at the bottom rung of the ladder, though. No one gave me any hand-outs. I had three jobs going at once to pay for even more education, and had to work to be accepted in society. Why should society trust me? My track record said it shouldn't. I had to eat a lot of humble pie in those days. I saw the beauty of life outside prison and wanted to take full advantage.

As I say, I'd met Lynn on the inside – she was the prison librarian, and we had spent hours discussing my poems about the treatment of inmates. She agreed with my plans to help ex-offenders go straight, through education.

Six months after my release, we were married at Maidstone Register Office. Lynn gave up her job so that we could be together. My new wife was one of the most honourable and decent people I'd ever met. However, I had entered her world with all its prejudices against ex-criminals, and the odds were stacked against us from the start. Even her mother and father refused to come to our wedding, although her grandmother, sister and brother were absolute diamonds. Even to this day I get on well with my ex-brother-in-law. We enjoyed a magnificent reception at the White Horse pub in East Farleigh near Maidstone.

We rented a small cottage and I was determined to live a crime-free life. But I soon found that I just was not welcome in this society. And I could also see how, when ex-offenders were rejected by 'decent' society, but welcomed by the society that had groomed them for a life of crime, many went back to their bad old ways.

I found that I was still locked in a world that revolved around the date when I was first arrested. One day, as I sat wondering how I would get a job and hating the prejudices out there, Lynn suggested that I should go out and explore our area, and have a few drinks with the locals.

'Phone me when you're ready to come home,' she said. 'It'll do you good, and I'll have dinner ready when you get back.'

It was a strange, strange experience. After being locked up for years, there I was, in a Victorian-style pub, wondering what to drink and how much it would cost. I knew that Charlie Richardson had similar problems: he told me he walked around with bags of change as he came to terms with the changeover from pounds, shillings and pence.

Decisions, decisions. What should I order to drink? In prison they make all the decisions for you. They decide when you should go to bed, when you should wake up and what you will eat each day. Then they release you, and you must make all those decisions yourself. If you make the wrong decisions, you end up back behind bars, and so the cycle continues.

With no crimes to concentrate on, I ditched the bitter lemon but still played it fairly safe with a half pint of lager. I was surprised at how much it cost. Seemed like a rip-off for fizzy yellow liquid.

I sat in the corner, watching the locals. Some nodded, and I nodded back. They were discussing betting odds, news in the papers and the best buys in the motors section. After another two halves I became bored and decided to call Lynn from the phone box outside the pub.

Well, I looked for the slot to put my money in, but there wasn't one. There was just a slot which looked as if it was designed for notes and all that. What? A fiver to make a call? Too embarrassed just to back out of there, I spoke into a silent phone, felt totally confused and made my way home.

As I walked back to the cottage I tried to work out the odd system in the phone box. In prison, if you wanted to make a call, the welfare officer made the connection for you.

'Why didn't you call?' Lynn asked as I arrived at the door. 'Didn't you find a phone box?'

'There's a slot for notes – it didn't take any change.'

'That's for a phone card!' She chuckled. 'Of course, you won't know what they are. Come with me.'

Lynn took me along to the local shop and bought me a phone card. I could now communicate with the outside world.

I was learning bits and pieces every day.

I sat in our little cottage writing out job application after job application. I sent out around 200 a week and received setback after setback. Some companies didn't even bother to reply.

I was totally honest about my past and went into all the details. However, no one offered me a job. On the other hand, our home telephone was ringing all the time with offers of employment from criminal gangs in London. We had no money, but I decided to plod on with my legal job hunting.

I grew more and more despondent and desperate as the weeks went by. *'Fuck this,'* I thought. *'Maybe I should go up to London and do a couple of jobs with the gangs.'* I knew that would sort us out financially, but Lynn would have none of it. And she was pregnant with our first child.

'It's either a life of crime, or me.'

To be fair, she'd given everything up for me, including her family. So I worked out a new tactic when going for jobs: I had to be dishonest when applying for an honest position! I used my London contacts to provide a list of building companies that had gone bust and closed down. I added the names to my CV, invented positions, and it did the trick.

I applied for a job as a night shelf-packer in Tesco and got it. It seemed to be a big step down from being the head of a criminal gang, with low pay and hard work, but at least it was an honest living.

My first evening, I had my sandwiches packed, my flask of tea ready, and off I went to my night job. I clicked with most of the staff straight away – all, apart from, that is, the night manager. He was a nightmare.

He was around twenty-one years old, and a real nobody trying to be somebody. He strutted around with a plastic folder under his arm, making a general pest of himself. He sucked up to the women, and tried to impress them by bullying the men.

I saw him for what he was, kept my head down and carried on with my work. I needed this job, but it wasn't long before he'd singled me out and gave me all the rubbish jobs to do. He picked on me for not putting on stickers properly, and showed me how quickly he could use a pricing gun.

I just thought, *'Don't worry about how fast you are with a pricing gun. Keep on going the way you're going and I'll show you how fast I am with a fucking shotgun.'*

I know what you're thinking: I wasn't at my 'turning point' just yet, despite my efforts to go totally straight.

I ignored the little wanker and grafted away for two months. I remember bringing home my first pay packet of £100. You would have thought that I had brought home the Crown Jewels. Lynn was so proud. We treated ourselves to fish and chips and a bottle of red wine. It wasn't the cuisine I'd been used to in my heyday, but fish and chips and red wine never tasted so good!

People who were involved in my business operations, during my crime years, had spent all of my cash. We're talking about a small fortune here – a large amount of money that had allowed me to enjoy the high life as a criminal. I had two choices: I could either go and shoot them and get the money back, or walk away and start a new life. I started that new life with Lynn, even though I'd come out with £1,800 to my name.

At work, however, the little jerk still would not leave me alone. One night I thought, *'Fuck you. People in here are in vulnerable positions, suffering all this because they need a crap job to feed their families. If you come on to me tonight, I am really going to educate you.'*

Sure enough, he failed to read the writing on the wall. It was there for him to read, but somehow he didn't see it. Somehow he failed to see the need for his own education ...

'Oi! You haven't shelved the dog food properly. Straighten those cans up. Why do I have to sort out your mistakes all the time?'

He walked away and I seized my chance. I followed right behind him, grabbed hold of the little creep and pushed him into the cold storage area. I could tell that he was frozen with fear.

I pressed him up against the wall, slapped his face and snarled, 'If you ever fuck with me or any of the others again, I will beat the fucking shit out of you and hang you up on that meat rack.'

I headed off to carry on with my routine tasks as the pathetic night manager ran upstairs to his office and locked the door. An hour later a security firm arrived, asked me to collect my gear and leave – otherwise they would call the Old Bill. The last thing I wanted was more aggravation, so I picked up my gear and headed off back home to Lynn.

I told her what had happened, and she was worried, but

thankfully the police hadn't been called in. I felt sorry for the effect it had on Lynn, but I had no regrets about actually threatening the little wanker. He deserved it.

The next morning I was summoned to the store and fired on the spot. I told them what had happened and, fortunately, the night crew backed up my story about the bullying. It didn't help my case, but at least I'd made my point. The night manager, however, was still frightened and asked to be transferred to another store.

My mate, Nick, was promoted to night manager. He had also been upset by the bullying tactics; he brought me round the wages due and a bottle of wine. Everyone felt the same as me, although I'd foolishly taken the law into my own hands. I'd brought those tactics from my manor and, on this occasion, I'd failed to win the day.

After a few weeks I had another job, selling advertising space in our local paper. Tony Williams was running that show as editor. He was a real Christian with a good heart and full of compassion. Tony is still a dear friend of mine and really is one of life's beautiful people.

I worked with Tony and his crew for a while, and then landed a job with a housing association. The manager was a woman called Pat Willet. She knew about my past, but she'd still hired me, bless her. And, as I'd be working at a hostel for ex-offenders, she thought that I would be an asset to the operation.

One day she called me into her office and said I was on call. That was an added bonus, as the on-call person worked during the day and carried a pager at night. You were paid for being on call and received extra money if you had a callout.

Pat knew I had a baby on the way and wanted to do her best by me. She was a real diamond who cared about the people in her care and would help anyone out. Her husband, Stewart, was the same.

After a while working for the association, Pat said one day: 'Here are the keys to all the buildings and the safe.'

I couldn't believe that Bobby Cummines, ex-bank robber, was being given all those keys! I said I didn't really want that responsibility in case anything went wrong: the last thing I wanted was for anyone to nick money from the safe, with the finger of suspicion pointed at me.

'You are now a member of staff and I trust you,' Pat told me. 'You're being treated the same as everyone else. Take the keys or leave the job.' I took the keys, and my time at that job lasted for a couple of years.

It helped to be working with an old friend from my past, Dave Smith, who came from South London and was a few years younger than me. His previous job had been working at a used car garage with a well-known South London villain. Dave and I worked well together and he became like a brother to me; even to this day, we are always there for each other. There's nothing I enjoy more than working in a comfortable environment with my own people.

Lynn and I plodded on and nature took its course. My daughter, Sophie, was born in 1990; I was so proud and possessive that I wouldn't let anyone hold her.

I cradled Sophie in my arms all the time. I took her out of her cot and into our bed all the time, and enjoyed feeling her breathing next to me. I would carry her for miles rather than have to put her in a pram. If members of my family – apart from my wife, of course – wanted to hold her I would resist. My Sophie was the most beautiful thing in my life and I didn't trust anyone with her. I knew that, with me, she was totally safe.

Even when Sophie was a teenager we would cuddle up on the sofa. If she had a problem with a boyfriend I would say, 'Tell me all about it.' Sophie was the jewel in my crown all the time – my life had been so ugly, and then Sophie came along, and my entire life revolved around her.

I knuckled down, earning as many crusts as I could, but tragedy was not far away.

No parent ever imagines that a child could die before them. Even if you meet another parent whose child has passed away, you never know how they really feel. We all deal with a tragedy in the best way we can. I have been shot, stabbed, imprisoned and left to rot; I lived through it all, but nothing prepared me for the death of Abigail. I'll brace myself and give you the story.

Everything was going so well, with the Tesco incident behind me and forgotten. I remained active in the jobs market and became stock control manager for a cash-and-carry company in Kent. Because I was so used to being 'the fixer' in prison, I found the job really easy. I saved them thousands of pounds by reorganising their systems – and then an electronics company heard about my way of working.

Yes, I was headhunted! They wanted me as their stock control manager. I made a deal with them: take me on for a month and, if I saved them money, they would employ me with a larger salary. If I failed, then I would walk away. I used the same finely honed techniques employed in the prison and at the cash-and-carry store, and saved them a small fortune.

Could life get any better for an ex-con? I adored tiny Sophie, and my wife Lynn was heavily pregnant again. Then, one day, the phone rang in my office. It was Mike, my next-door neighbour. 'They've taken Lynn into hospital. The baby must be due any time ... you'd better get home as quickly as you can.'

I had been expecting the news. After all, Lynn was due to give birth at any time and we were all looking forward to welcoming a new brother or sister for Sophie.

I didn't drive at the time, and so the warehouse manager took me home. I was packing bags for Lynn and bits and bobs for myself when the phone rang. It was one of the senior nurses.

'Mr Cummines, could you come to the hospital straight away? Your wife needs you.'

The taxi couldn't come quickly enough. I could tell from the nurse's voice that something was seriously wrong. I feared the worst but, as the taxi sped towards the hospital, I couldn't get my head around what the worst could be. Was there something abnormal about the child?

I entered the private room, saw my wife's face and knew that my baby was dead. I sat with Lynn for a while and then went to the hospital chapel to see Abigail. There she was, resting in a small wicker basket. Tears flowed down my face and my head felt like it would explode at any moment. I could hardly breathe.

'Can I be of any help? Would you like to talk? Perhaps you will pray with me.'

'Fuck off,' I snarled at the priest. 'Do you want me to nail you up alongside your guv'nor?'

OK. I should never have said that. But I had caught a whiff of booze on the priest's breath; I thought he was just going through the motions as he didn't know me, and I wanted to be left alone. To be fair to the priest, he shot off out the chapel and left me to my misery.

After a few minutes of reflection, I stomped out of the chapel and into the car park.

'*Why have you done this?*' I tried to reason with God. '*I even packed shelves in a supermarket. I didn't have any money, but refused to go back into crime. Why the fuck have you done this to us?*'

Swearing at God was a poor response, and I asked for his forgiveness. I also asked him to forgive me for slagging off the priest.

I walked slowly back towards the hospital. The sky was dark and an eerie cloak hid the stars. I approached the hospital's main doors and saw they were locked for the night. I went in through a side entrance that took me on a different route to my wife's room. I passed the windows of the baby intensive care unit and looked in to see beautiful angels with their parents standing guard. Those people were drained of all energy, crying and filled with fear.

I could see that other parents were about to follow my route to hell, while others would be spared that horrendous journey. I was not alone; I could see that clearly. All those people with the same nightmares gave me comfort; I had a daughter on Earth and another in Heaven, waiting for me.

The beautiful babies of this world are our future and we should nurture and cherish them because they really are our priceless jewels.

I still feel that Abigail is with me. I can sense her presence all around. Grieving sent me into a place I didn't want to visit, fuelled by too much alcohol. My behaviour wrecked my marriage. The break-up and subsequent divorce in 1998 were entirely down to me.

So, what to do for Abigail? I made a promise to turn things around completely and dedicate my work to her – but how would I go about it?

Back in civvy street, after all my hassles on the job front, I was determined to fulfil that promise to Abigail. I heard about a bloke who was starting up an organisation called Unlock – it was brought to my attention by Maurice, my old probation officer from Maidstone who'd done so much for me in the past. I was intrigued.

I contacted the founder, Mark, and arranged a meeting with him in London. When we met, I had the shock of my life.

It was Mark Leech, a fellow ex-inmate at Maidstone. Although also classed as a problem prisoner, he was well educated and knew more about prison rules than any barrister.

In fact, he was every prison governor's nightmare. In prison, he had helped people to write about their complaints and was known to us as the prison 'lawyer'. Mark and I had a good laugh and he told me about his scheme to help ex-offenders live a normal life outside prison, with all the training, rehabilitation and counselling that went with it.

I knew from his determination and commitment in prison that he would give it a real go. Funding was the main issue, so we set about getting a structure in place. As it was Mark's idea, it was only right that he should be in charge, with me as his deputy.

We worked night and day to get the project off the ground: we were in and out of TV and radio stations up and down the country. It nearly killed us both – Mark was in poor health anyway, which only added to the strain on him.

Unlock was a charity run by ex-offenders for ex-offenders. Our message: 'We live that life that others can only guess about; and we are living in an unforgiving and sometimes brutal society that is not willing to give us a break.'

From my garage we applied for grants to the Tudor Trust and the Wates Foundation. That helped us to run a proper office and paid us a salary, too, so that we could look at our positions as full-time jobs. These two charities totally supported us for many years, which allowed us then to really set the wheels in motion.

We did it. Unlock became a respected charity, run by ex-offenders for ex-offenders. We began with £6 and ended up with a turnover of £100,000 a year. As time went on we had to employ more staff, and the charity was finding it harder to pay for everything. But we just kept going, against all the odds.

Mark was excellent at dealing with the media, solicitors and everyone. He wrote articles in newspapers, outlining the problems facing ex-offenders and putting forward a compelling case. The next thing, we were getting phone calls from TV and radio stations asking us to comment on what was happening in prisons and the problems of adapting to life on the outside.

We had to prepare for all these interviews: we made sure we said all the right things, we were always armed with the right statistics, and we put our points across in an articulate way. Mark and I handled all the media ourselves, and it was a 24/7 operation.

Not only was my business life taking off, but so was my personal life. I met Ami in a club in the mid-1990s. Her husband, Paul, was a roadie for a heavy metal band. He was a lovely guy and they had a young son, Kai. Sadly, Paul died from pneumonia when Kai was only six years old.

Paul's family came from Newcastle; my Ami is the only Japanese bird I know who speaks with a Geordie accent. I lost touch with her for a long time until I went onto Facebook around 2004, six years after my divorce. I was just chatting to people on there when she popped up, and I started asking her what was happening in her life.

We started talking and became really good friends. She was in Japan at the time, and I invited Ami and Kai to come to visit me in Kent. They came and we all spent Christmas together.

Things just developed from there. The next time they came over, Ami and I started talking about the future. I just knew that this woman was the only one that I ever wanted.

I said, 'Look, Ami, we get on good and we aren't kids any more. What do you think about us getting married?'

She answered, 'What are you saying to me?'

'I'm saying, will you marry me?'

Ami's pretty face looked at me quizzically: 'Are you serious?'

I told her in no uncertain terms: 'Yes, I don't talk to give my mouth exercise.'

There was quiet in the room and then, after a while, she said, 'If you are serious then yes, OK.'

And that was it.

When the media first came to us at Unlock, they thought they would be dealing with mindless thugs who, they presumed, wouldn't be articulate or a match for MPs and so-called specialists in prison life. 'What do these people know about after-care for prisoners?' seemed to be their general approach.

We wiped the floor with the lot of them. Mark and I were well read, we'd studied our subject, we'd lived the prison life and we were confident during interviews. Also, the MPs and specialists couldn't get away with telling lies; we knew the truth, whereas they were only guessing.

It soon became obvious to the journalists and the media in general that our firebrand approach was being well received by listeners, viewers and readers. They couldn't get enough of us. Unlock was seen as a force to be reckoned with in print and on the radio.

We became familiar names on Radio 4, Sky, ITV and the BBC when we went to town about prison overcrowding and all that. As well as news stories, we took part in documentaries and televised conferences. We became keynote speakers and, I feel, deserved our place on the airwaves.

On the personal front, my mother-in-law, bless her, came over from Japan for our wedding in 2008 despite being poorly. She stayed with us for a few weeks and we took her around all the places she wanted to visit. We all got on really well. I really did like my mother-in-law.

Japanese people are very family orientated. To start with Ami's family were understandably concerned about my background and everything that they read about me on the internet. Ami told them that was all in the past and I now ran a charity for ex-prisoners.

Our marriage itself was a quiet affair. It really was a private do at the Archbishop's Palace in Maidstone. Only close friends and family attended.

Japanese people are totally respectful and law abiding

and I wanted my son to grow up in that environment. I was glad that Kai had taken on a lot of Japanese values; in fact, he preferred those to the English way of life.

Kai travelled all the way from Chatham in Kent to his Japanese school at East Acton in London every day. That was quite a commitment for a twelve year old, on top of his school work. He appreciated that I paid his fees, and he rewarded us with good qualifications. Ami and I always attended parents' evenings and any plays he was in. We wanted him to know that he was fully supported and loved.

When Kai finished the Japanese school in London, aged fifteen, he was due to go to a sixth-form college. However, I'd been lecturing at schools in London where I saw glue sniffing, kids being robbed of their mobile phones and trainers, and many of them carrying an assortment of weapons. Kai is a gentle soul and I didn't want him exposed to those horrors. I'd grown up with all of that and knew what would be coming his way. The only way I could achieve that was to send him to a school in Japan where crime was almost zero and respect for others was top of the agenda.

We applied to the Doshi School in Japan; it was an expensive option, but the right one. All the money from my criminal years had gone, but I'd worked hard since my release and ploughed the proceeds into Kai's education. I raised funds, giving advice on security and carrying out lots of media work. Kai had to sit various tests to ensure that he could cope with the high standards expected of him.

Normally most men who marry a woman with children see the kids as baggage. I didn't see Kai as that; I saw him as the son I chose to have. In my mind Kai is my son. At the same time, I maintained a really close relationship with my daughter Sophie, who was developing into a fantastic young woman. Yes, I really did have everything going for me. Everything.

CHAPTER FIFTEEN

PRACTISING WHAT I PREACHED

As Mark's health deteriorated, he thought it best to stand down and hand the organisation over to me. Not long after this, our first president, Judge Stephen Tumim, died, and Sir David Ramsbotham (later to become Lord Ramsbotham) stepped in to take his place.

I liked David from the first moment I met him in his role as Chief Inspector of Prisons. He was an old general with good principles and a strong sense of what was right and fair. He was like a Rottweiler with the heart of a lion. Judge John Samuels, another absolute diamond, acted as vice-president. We had other high-profile patrons who were strong voices in our organisation and provided solid advice for the government.

With Lord Ramsbotham's backing, I took Unlock to another level, making it a charity that most admired and some envied. I had turned it into a 'doing' charity, unlike others that were just talking shops. I carried on appearing in all the media, and went into schools to give talks on deglamorising crime.

I was invited to sit on many government think tanks and committees. I was appointed specialist advisor to the House of Commons Home Affairs Committee on the Rehabilitation of Offenders Act chaired by John Denham MP. I was also a member of the Deputy Prime Minister's Advisory Committee.

I pressed on with my plans as chief executive of Unlock. I had so many issues to tackle. Prisoners stood no chance of living a normal life on the outside.

I discovered that, if you let someone with a criminal record live in your house, your home contents and building insurance became invalid. People had been paying out thousands to insurance companies without knowing this. Insurance brokers Roy Clegg and Nick Graham campaigned on my behalf and, lo and behold, policies were changed to reflect our requests.

How do ex-offenders get jobs? I used my own example of how to do it, but I had bent the rules on my application forms. I managed to find jobs for some former prisoners, but more obstacles appeared. Employers said they couldn't employ ex-criminals because staff were paid through the BACS system and former prisoners usually didn't have bank accounts because they were ex-offenders. Outrageous! They wanted to take people on, but couldn't pay them!

To make matters worse, prisoners leaving jail received their benefits by giro and could only collect their money from their local post office on a certain day. This was dangerous for women ex-prisoners, often with violent, abusive partners who would prowl around the post office waiting for the cash. With the help of Barry, a financial expert, and Morag from the Bank of Scotland, we changed all of that. Following our success with insurance, we started on a small scale with bank accounts. While inside doing my bird, I'd handled all the deals and financial stuff, so I just continued that work, legally, on the outside. Soon all the banks came on board. Job done.

Unlock really took off at the start of the new millennium. To start with, the organisation was known as 'the gangsters' union'. People in politics, newspapers, the police and everyone said we would be involved in organised crime. They said it was a front for the British underworld, similar to the Krays' plans to have a Mafia-style operation in England. The Old Bill said I was slippery and always covered my tracks. I even heard that there were fears about us corrupting politicians. I was more worried about politicians corrupting us.

Unlock wasn't a front for anything apart from helping our own people. The Establishment was shocked when they discovered that we were legit. We made fools of all of them.

There had never been a charity run by ex-offenders for ex-offenders. Normally the charities helping former prisoners were made up of middle- or upper-class people doing the Lord's work. Other charities helping ex-offenders were more in the business of helping themselves into employment and justifying their own miserable existences. I'm not saying that they were all bad people – far from it. They just didn't understand what the ex-offender, trying to go straight, was going through.

It's a case of reading a book on how to make bread but not putting your hands in the dough. What you had was a lot of theory but no practical experience of that type of life. They had very few ex-offenders – if any – working for them. With those that did, the ex-offender had a very low status within the organisation: they didn't hold management positions and couldn't influence policy or the ethos of the charity.

We were very well received at the conference table. In fact, the National Offender Management Service asked me to be the keynote speaker at their major conference to lift the morale of their staff. People there were so down, always being criticised by the media, and I tried to give them a bit of a lift. Public speaking came naturally to me. I was never nervous, as I was full of confidence and knew my subject off by heart.

I believe I was in the right place at the right time to push for reform. We'd had prison riots over the years; the problems of re-offending, over and over; the recognised need to prevent prisoners going back inside; and the mountain of problems facing prisoners who wanted to go straight. Leading figures in the police, the judiciary and politics were looking for a way forward and I was able to lead the way. I was asked to sit on more government panels looking at the rehabilitation of prisoners. I was invited to join the House of Lords Select Committee dealing with disabled prisoners. I found myself on a wide selection of committees between 1999 and 2010. I even advised the board of HM Chief Inspector of Prisons.

I was always checking to see if prisoners who posed no threat at all could be integrated back into the community. For example, I knew the late Bruce Reynolds well. Bruce masterminded the Great Train Robbery and we were both concerned about the health of Ronnie Biggs. Ronnie had had strokes and all that, and was no longer a danger to society.

I campaigned to have Ronnie freed, and he was eventually released on compassionate grounds. Ronnie died at the age of eighty-four while I was completing this book.

We were a non-political organisation, so had no prejudice or favour towards any party. We told it as it was, which made all political parties respect us.

I asked the Conservative MP Edward Garnier and Lib Dem Nick Clegg MP to support me in my aims to build a training campus for reformed offenders. They both gave me their full support. Coutts Bank took care of the launch and donated £10,000 to Unlock. The newspapers had a field day with that one, especially when Perry Littleboy, one of the Coutts directors, handed over the cheque. Perry said he was pleased to see me in his bank without a crash helmet and a gun.

Perry and the other directors of Coutts provided massive support and guidance. They introduced me to potential funders and I will always be indebted to them for that. I will always hold them in the highest esteem.

I made sure that people knew I detested sexism, racism or any other fucking new-fangled 'isms'. In my book, the bottom line is whether you are a good or a bad person. One time, when I was lecturing to prisoners at Rochester Young Offenders Institution, I was talking to some mates and I saw a guy talking over everyone. He wouldn't let anyone ask any questions. He was a one-man fucking crowd.

I told the loud, loud prisoner to be quiet and give the others a chance to speak.

'You don't like me because I'm black,' he muttered.

'I don't like you because you are fucking rude and I wouldn't like you if you were white, either,' I hit back. Everyone in the room started clapping and cheering.

'Sorry, man, I got that one wrong,' he apologised with a big grin.

He came up to me afterwards and told me that I was a star. I'm glad he did, because he was six feet tall and built like a brick shithouse. I told him not to play the race card because, when it really happened, people wouldn't believe it. I said it was just like crying wolf. It's the same when people say they are tortured in prison and it hasn't really happened. That undermines the torture when it really happens, so it's best never to cry wolf.

I went into prisons all over the UK – it's one part of the work I enjoy the most. I said that I reckoned most of the inmates were in there for under £500, which meant they were doing a five-year stretch for a profit of around £100 a year. I told them that they were better off on the dole.

I said to one guy who was doing bird for drugs: 'When you got your gear, did you test it to make sure it was good?'

'Yes, I did,' he said.

'Well, that is quality control, so that is important. When you sold the gear, did you have a look at the best areas to sell it in?'

'Yes, we had a tour around to find the most likely areas,' he admitted.

'Well, that is distribution networking,' I confirmed. 'And, in those areas, did you find out where you would get the best prices?'

'Yes, we had that sorted.'

'You have all the skills of a manager,' I pointed out. 'Only problem is, you were selling the wrong product.'

Shortly afterwards, the guy was released and I bumped into him, doing window cleaning.

'I listened to what you said,' he grinned. 'I'm now running a little window cleaning company along with two people who were in the nick with me.'

I then bumped into him again in Westminster, running a car valeting firm. He had his own van and employed a few others to clean cars.

'Do you know of any window cleaning jobs going, Bobby? Anyone need a car cleaned? We have all the skills!'

I told his story when I went back into the prisons. His mates were flabbergasted, because previously he'd always been in and out of jail.

From prisons to parliaments, I went to a lot of places to spread the word. I was invited over to Dublin to talk to the Irish government about putting together a Rehabilitation of Offenders Act, as they didn't have one. I gave a series of talks over there about my ideas to prevent prisoners going back inside.

I travelled to India to see how organised crime was evolving out there. The Chinese government invited me, too, to study operations run by the Triads and to advise on combating organised crime.

Best of all was my trip to South Africa in 2006, sponsored by Garden Court Chambers, a firm of solicitors in Holborn, to see how prisons there were run. I met members of the ANC, and we compared South African prisons with British jails.

We also studied the South African judicial system. That was a real eye-opener, because the people running the judiciary were once prisoners themselves under apartheid laws. Because of their understanding of what it was like to be a prisoner, they had a deep understanding of discrimination; they also knew what it was like to be released, facing life with the label of a criminal.

I stayed with Chantal Fortuin and her husband, Lloyd, who were once high-ranking ANC people, close to Mandela. Chantal is now a High Court judge, and Lloyd is one of their top human rights lawyers. I stayed with them and their little family and met numerous people who had fought with Nelson Mandela and Walter Sisulu during the struggles against apartheid. It's hard to believe that Chantal was handcuffed to her bed while she gave birth to her son, due to the ANC's terrorist status during the apartheid years. I still can't get my head around that one.

Chantal and Lloyd had both done bird on Robben Island in Table Bay, the same prison where Mandela was imprisoned for eighteen of his twenty-seven years behind bars. The couple took me to the island and it sent shivers down my spine. The Atlantic Ocean hammers against the rocks and you can see why so many ships have foundered there. The evil place was used to house political prisoners as long ago as the end of the seventeenth century. The island had also been a leper colony, so I didn't fancy hanging around for too long. When I visited the island, I met several caretakers who were once prisoners with Nelson Mandela.

Chantal and Lloyd knew that I had completed a lengthy sentence which meant that we had a unique bond. In fact, I always refer to the couple as my South African family.

I visited all the prisons in South Africa, from young offenders' institutions to high-security jails. I talked to inmates, guards and their Inspector of Prisons. I noticed that most of the prisons were farm-based and contained a high proportion of young people. They got up early in the morning to work on the farm; their produce was sent to poor shanty towns, and that really impressed me. They weren't banged up for twenty-three hours a day, as in British jails, and they were carrying out useful activities, helping the wider community. I brought these ideas back to the UK.

South Africa had the same problems as the UK: drug addiction, prostitution and armed robberies. However, they were proactive in dealing with the issues, looking for rehabilitation rather than simply punishment.

My travels weren't only for the charity. After Kai had been at the Doshi School for a while, we decided to fly out to Japan to see him and check how well he was settling in.

I had no idea what to expect. Being married to someone from a different country and culture is truly an eye opener. Though I love my wife and son Kai with all my heart, I knew nothing about Japan, or its culture and customs. Meeting my in-laws was going to be an exciting experience for me, too.

I remember getting on the plane with Ami. I was too excited to sleep and watched the films on the headrest in front of me. Occasionally, I glanced over at my wife and thought how stunning she was. Ami is no good at taking compliments; when I tell her she is gorgeous she tells me to shut up.

A flood of thoughts flashed through my head. *Would they like me? How would I talk to them? I didn't speak any Japanese; what would they make of my Cockney accent?* I'd met my sister-in-law, Yukari, and got on well with her. She was an air hostess and spoke perfect English, so there was no problem there, but my brother-in-law, Ma, and other sister-in-law, Mika, spoke very little English. But I knew that I could depend on Ami and Kai to bail me out if communication became a problem.

We arrived in Japan in the late afternoon and met up with our Kai. I needn't have worried about my first meeting with the family. I found them all to be truly lovely people. Ma and I got on like a house on fire. I also got on well with Yukari's husband. My little Japanese nieces, Lilika and

Reku, were really sweet children. In fact, I could not ask for a better family of in-laws than I have now in Japan.

I have always admired the respectful attitude and honesty of the Japanese people. Nothing is too much trouble for them to make a stranger feel comfortable in their country or home; this is something that we seem to have lost today in Britain.

Ami and Kai wanted me to see everything in our local area and so we went on adventures to the shopping malls and games arcades, all trying to win prizes and fluffy toys. Ami and Kai were experts on the machines and won prize after prize. There were also restaurants where you could fish and catch your own lunch. Ami and Kai have done that, but I've still to give it a try. Kai has a wicked sense of humour and loved teasing me by giving me Japanese food, knowing that I found it disgusting. He tried to make me eat funny-tasting soups and fish with chillies, and laughed as I spat it out. My favourite place to eat was Mister Donut. They have every type of doughnut under the rising sun. English doughnuts can make you feel as if you are chewing on a brick, but the Japanese versions are light and fluffy.

The temples are amazing places to visit. They store and display sacred Buddhist objects, and there are thousands of the ornate buildings throughout the country.

I was most impressed by the cleanliness of Japan: the streets were spotless, the railway stations were perfect, trains ran on time and the guards on the carriages wore white gloves. They were polite and always willing to help.

Walking with my wife among the cherry blossom and temples gave me beautiful memories that only we will share. They will stay with me for the rest of my life.

I love Japan because the country gave me Ami, a son and my extended Japanese family. I am proud that Ami entrusted me with her future and that of her son. It is the biggest leap of faith that anyone can make, and I am determined to do my best for them. I don't just love my beautiful wife; I am in love with her also because she stands by me through the good and bad times. I do the same for her.

Back in the UK, I was appointed as specialist advisor to Mr Justice Keith for the case of the murder of nineteen-year-old Zahid Mubarik by his cell-mate in Feltham Young Offenders' Institution. Mr Justice Keith compiled a 700-page report. He concluded that the professional failings of nineteen members of the Prison Service had led, in some way, to the death. Zahid died at the hands of racist Robert Stewart, who beat him with a table leg. Stewart, who had 'RIP' and a cross tattooed on his forehead, was destined to kill.

Justice Keith taught me so many things. He showed me how to record evidence and how to challenge witnesses. He showed me exactly how an inquiry works; I learned from the horse's mouth.

One day at the inquiry, during recess, I told him, 'Do you realise that most of my life I've been standing in front of judges awaiting sentence and now, Justice Keith, I'm sitting by your side advising you?'

'What a strange world,' he replied. 'You know, you could write a book about that.'

While I was advising him, he asked me if I thought it would be a good idea to put a young person in with someone who is doing a big sentence, like a lifer.

'Not in a million years,' I told him.

'Why is that?' Justice Keith asked.

'Because they will groom him,' I explained. 'If you put a young person in with maximum-security prisoners who are career criminals, they will use him. They will convert him. Tell you what I'll do – come with me, and I'll show you how it's done.'

So we went into a high-security prison and we saw a young kid who was in for burglary. The first thing I had to do was explain to my learned friend all about the different types of prisoners; who would do the grooming, and who wouldn't have a clue.

Justice Keith told the kid all about my previous life and I went to work. I quickly sussed out that this kid was in for non-violent offences. He'd been nicked for burglary and doing a bit of puff.

'So, when you get visits, do your girlfriend and family come and bring you cash and presents?' I asked the raw, nervous kid.

'Yes, they visit me regularly,' he answered, wondering where this was going.

'So, imagine that you are in a cell with me. I know you are non-violent and I can bully you. I can take all your goodies from you. There are some nasty people in here. I send someone in to give you a clump, but I stop them doing it, and now I am your friend.'

The kid pursed his lips, looked at Justice Keith, and turned his attention back to me.

'So now I am your friend and you get your regular visits. I see photos of your girlfriend up on your board. I've got one of your letters so I know where she lives. Now I want her to bring in a parcel for me. It starts off with a few quid. Your girlfriend does that because otherwise I'll beat the crap out of you.'

The kid twitched nervously as he started getting the picture.

'If you do this for me, I tell you I'll make you very rich when you come out. You can come on the firm with us because I know I can trust you.'

The kid nodded, taking it all in.

'The next parcel that comes in will be drugs. You've already smuggled stuff in, so it doesn't matter. If your girlfriend doesn't co-operate, I can get someone to visit her on the outside. So now I've got you. You are in my firm, and I've got you.'

The kid nodded again and I said to Justice Keith, 'You see what I mean?'

As we were walking away the kid said: 'Oi, Bobby, I've done an armed robbery, too.'

They brought a lifer out to see us. He was in for killing his old woman. As I said earlier, most men and women who are in for murder are what we call 'red mist' killers. They are in an abusive relationship, have never committed a crime before, and will never commit a crime again. Pushed too far, the red mist comes down, they top their partner. But they are not a danger to anyone else.

This guy knew nothing about crime. Although he had committed a heinous offence, he was not involved in organised crime. He'd just had that one moment of madness. That is why we should have alternative offences for people, like they do in France for crimes of passion.

Justice Keith said he had had to see all that with his own eyes to believe it.

'That's not a problem because you've taught me a lot of things,' I pointed out. 'I've shown you a perspective you could never see. That is why you can never put young, impressionable people in with professional criminals.'

I told him that hardened villains should be housed in a special prison so that this grooming couldn't happen, and low-tariff offenders should be kept somewhere else. I stressed that mixing people just led to that example of the kid being persuaded to continue a life of crime.

I had the greatest respect for Justice Keith and still hold him in the highest esteem. I showed him a side of prison that he did not know about; he showed me how to handle the inquiry with a firm, just hand. He gave justice to the Mubarik family, and I am sure that would not have happened with other chairmen.

*

While I was chief executive of Unlock, I met a policeman as he was walking on the beat near my home in Snodland, near Maidstone. He said he was worried about drugs, knives and all that. He said the children needed to know what it was really like to be involved in a life of crime.

'I deal with ex-offenders in prison,' I told him. 'I've never done schools.'

'Would you give it a try?' he asked. 'If you get to them before they commit crimes and end up in prison, it would be a lot better, wouldn't it?'

'That makes sense,' I agreed. 'I'll give it a go.'

'They're a bit of a handful,' he warned.

'That's all right. No problem,' I assured him.

It was all approved with the relevant authorities, and so I went to work in the local schools. There was no political correctness with the kids: they were straight on to me, wanting to know what it was like to be shot. They needed to know what it was like to carry a gun, and I told them everything. I treated them as equals and shared all the information.

I laid it on the line about drugs: 'Some of you will have seen drugs. Some of you will have been tempted to use them. Remember that they are not prepared by a chemist. It's just a dealer putting a mix together, so who knows what is in the stuff.'

I held up a £10 note and asked them what it was. They confirmed that it was a £10 note. 'That is how much your life is worth to a drug dealer. Once he has your tenner, he doesn't care if you have a bad bit of gear that will kill you. If you have a bit of gear that doesn't work, he will adjust the mix. You are his guinea pigs. He is testing the gear out on you lot. You are paying to see if he has the mix right.'

The children sat with open mouths and said nothing.

'Sometimes you get brain damage and sometimes you're dead. You don't realise the grief you leave behind when you're dead. Think about your parents and the people who love you.'

It went down well with the police, because they knew only too well what I was talking about.

My other angle was to stress the dangers and stupidity of carrying knives, guns and other weapons.

Many of the kids I spoke to were carrying weapons and didn't realise the gravity of what they were doing. Word spread and we had loads of letters wanting me to go to more schools. I worked in as many as possible and even went to private ones. I made a slogan up: 'Mugs take drugs and fools carry tools.' The kids repeated it after me and that was a result.

After a constructive question and answer session, the entire class agreed that they should never carry weapons or be associated with anyone who carried them.

I was horrified to learn about the statistics for knife crime in London. In July 2013, I read that 1,000 people were victims of knife crime in the capital every month. The staggering statistic is that, in the first four months of 2013, eleven people were murdered in knife attacks in London.

Around 400 were injured and many others threatened. A lot of those injuries were serious and life-changing.

It's no consolation to me that the speed of the London Air Ambulance and the skill of surgeons are saving more lives. Those lives should never be put at risk in the first place, which is why my campaign to teach schoolchildren the rights and wrongs of it all will continue.

Glasgow, my friend Paul Ferris's stamping ground, is Britain's most violent city, according to the UK Peace Index, with London and Belfast second and third. I read the newspapers every day and haven't been impressed with the sentences handed out. A large number of offenders only receive a caution, an absolute or conditional discharge, or a fine.

No, I would not send them to jail. What is the use of that? They would come out, brutalised by the system and even more violent, ready to strike again. If I had my way they would be force-fed a regime, similar to my routine in the classroom, until the message got through. They would go through a strict rehabilitation programme at a training centre. I would take them to see the families devastated by the use of weapons, and I would make them pay compensation to the victims.

One incident comes to mind, when I went head to head with Home Secretary Jack Straw on Radio 4. The government wanted to build three massive jails holding 2,500 prisoners apiece, rather than consider spending money on rehabilitation. During the Radio 4 interview, I pointed out the dangers of overcrowding. Imagine a riot in one of those! Where would the dangerous prisoners go? The public would be put at serious risk.

During the programme I also pointed out to Jack, using Home Office statistics, that prisoners had committed at least three offences other than the one they were inside for. I asked him if he agreed. He said he did.

'So,' I replied, 'taking that as a yardstick, Jack, you are telling the public that, with these jails, you have catered for another 30,000 crimes to happen. If they cater for up to 10,000 prisoners, and each will have committed around another three offences, that is another 30,000 victims of crime.' I was pointing out that all those additional offences are taken into consideration, but the offender is not convicted of them. I confronted him with the figures and went on about the extra 30,000 victims of crime. I stressed that one extra victim of crime was one too many. And I couldn't see the point of incarcerating these people time after time when surely rehabilitation was the answer.

He wasn't keen on my figures, but I pressed home the point that I was using his statistics and not mine.

I kept on: 'But the ethos of a Titan jail is actually saying that. Are we talking about human warehousing, or rehabilitation? A prisoner should be coming out of jail rehabilitated, so that there are no more victims of crime.'

My argument was that the money should be spent, not on massive new Titan jails, but on educating prisoners and integrating them back into society.

The interviewer had a little snigger. When the programme ended, Jack said to me, 'That was a bit below the belt, Bobby!'

I replied, 'Your stats – not mine, Jack!'

Within months, the idea of Titan jails went onto the back burner – and disappeared. Jack and I have great respect for each other, and I am sure he will do me over during our next sparring contest.

He always highlighted the importance of punishing offenders; I continued to highlight the need to help them to go straight and stop offending. To be fair, Mr Straw does agree that the criminal justice system needs to give people the chance to turn their lives around, with a lot of the responsibility on the offender to seize opportunities. At the time of writing he's still active with his ideas and I have the greatest respect for him.

As my work in schools continued, Baroness Newlove – before she was Baroness Newlove – accompanied me. Her husband, Garry, was murdered after confronting a gang of drunken youths. He caught them vandalising her car; the rabble kicked him repeatedly in the head and were nicked for murder. The couple had three young daughters, and it was such a tragedy for the family. Helen Newlove, as she was then, painted the perfect picture of what it was like to be a victim of crime.

I stood in front of the classes and asked the kids if they had been with people who carried weapons. Loads of them put their hands up. Many of them also said they had seen assaults with weapons.

'It's a way of life around here,' one girl told me. 'Everyone carries a weapon for protection.'

I explained that a guy carrying a weapon was thirty-three times more likely to be a victim of violent crime. And I said that, when an attacker jumped out of a car to cut the guy, the girl would be carved up as well.

'Remember that, when people come looking for you, they will have weapons, too.'

Headmasters told me that kids were still going around saying: 'Mugs take drugs and fools carry tools.' It made me feel on top of the world and top of the class.

I could see that re-education wasn't only needed in schools, however. I noticed that with many television programmes about crime – especially documentaries – the emphasis was on blood and guts and violence. Everyone likes reading a good crime book with all the gory details, or seeing things acted out on TV. My mission was to cover all of that, of course, but also to include stories like the guy who came out of prison, went straight, became educated and found a good job. Those good news stories weren't sexy enough, but I battled on and had them covered, too.

More in-depth programmes followed, and my solo career took off. TV stations wanted to know all about the criminal underworld and how on earth a dangerous man like me could be rehabilitated. One of the companies with a feel for the subject was Talent South East, run by Kate Beal. There I met Fred Dinenage, a legend on TV and an expert on the operations of criminal gangs.

When Unlock won the *Guardian* Charity of the Year award in 2011, we had the opportunity to send three people to the ceremony. Two of the staff, plus me, were due to receive the award from Jane Asher. I pretended I was sick and couldn't attend the event. I put names in a hat and picked out three of them.

The *Guardian* took a picture of Jane Asher and my three workers; they deserved their day because they had done all the work. I believe that is how staff should be treated and rewarded.

Just thinking about that day and the award fills me with pride.

CHAPTER SIXTEEN
THE MIDAS TOUCH

When Ami's mum became seriously ill with cancer, we flew out to Japan as much as possible to be with her. We would get up in the morning and spend the whole day in hospital with her. I returned to England to sort out some pressing business while Ami stayed in Japan with her mother.

One night I was sitting watching the TV when the phone rang. It was Ami. 'You'd better get over here because Mother is not very good.'

'I'll be on my way.'

I brought Ami's mum a little doll from England because she collected that sort of thing. She wouldn't let anyone take it away from her. She looked so frail with tubes and all that coming out of her. My Japanese family are as strong as they come. They all surrounded Ami's mum with their love. I had to return to England for business reasons and during that time my mother-in-law died.

Her death really cut me up because she was one of the most beautiful people you could ever wish to meet. She was buried at Mount Fuji with her husband, who had died previously.

*

Although Unlock was having success out in the field, I didn't like the way things were going in the office. The charity was growing rapidly, but I had the impression that the admin staff – mostly straight-goers – had no real idea about the plight of prisoners or ex-offenders. They were reading all about it and guessing, which was no match for those who had lived it all. I wanted to change lives, not write essays.

Don't get me wrong. Unlock is still going and I wish them all the best for the future. It's just that I had a vision of ex-offenders and academics combining to move the organisation forward, and that did not seem to be happening.

Eventually, I moved on from Unlock because the charity was moving away from my original concept. People were phoning up and asking if their kid had to be a criminal to benefit from the scheme. Unlock was more of a policy thing, rather than being on the ground with the people. I wanted to be working at the coalface. I needed to be totally hands on.

I sat down and I thought about an idea I was calling 'Midas'. I'd been working on a project for about six years, and I thought that I needed to build and expand that idea.

I talked to Paul Ferris, who led a colourful life up in Scotland and is the subject of *The Wee Man* film about crime in Glasgow. He knew all about violence, kids being dragged into street gangs, drug abuse, people coming out of jail with no work and all that. I said we had the same problem down south and maybe we should go into partnership.

'We could call it Midas, build a Midas Centre and give the whole thing the Midas touch,' I told him.

'I like the sound of that,' Paul said. 'Let's get together.'

I'd already talked to Charlie Richardson about my plan, shortly before his death. Charlie had been concerned about kids in South London carrying guns and weapons, meaning that the streets were not at all safe. He also had problems in his own family and he was trying to sort those out.

'We need to get them before they go to jail,' Charlie stressed. 'Once they go to jail, we've lost them. When they're in jail they get educated in crime, as we know only too well.'

And so Charlie Richardson, Paul and I set up the Midas Charity. We had a meeting in Charlie's house in the summer of 2012. However, a couple of weeks later Charlie, bless his heart, became ill and passed on. We were just about to launch the project when he died.

I was devastated to hear about the death of Charlie Richardson.

More than 200 people attended the service at Honor Oak Crematorium in Brockley, South London. The least I could do was to handle the security, and I'm told it was like a military operation.

The arrangements, from flowers to invitations, were handled by Charlie's wife, Ronnie. Photographs were not allowed; only the official photographer could take pictures.

When I look back, I think of Charlie building up his scrapyard business, finding this and that of value in the craters during and after the war. It was a few years before I did the same thing, and when we talked about post-war London we shared very similar memories.

I made the following speech at the funeral:

'We are all here today to show our respects and support for Charlie and his family. I am not going to go into Charlie's past. We know the media will do that but, as we all know, what happened to Charlie, Eddie, Frankie Fraser and the others was one of the gravest miscarriages of justice in legal history. It was based on lies, fantasy and corruption perpetrated by the state.

'We all know Charlie was no angel, but he certainly was not the demon that the media and others would like to portray him as.

'I would like to talk about the Charlie I knew. He was a dear friend, a tutor and a highly sophisticated businessman.

'Charlie taught me many things when we served time together in Parkhurst while I was serving double figures for armed robbery.

'Up until the time I met Charlie, my life was totally committed to crime and violence – as was the case for most of us here today. Charlie saw something in me that, at that time in my life, I did not see myself. Charlie was really switched on to people. He could look at them and know their strengths, weaknesses and potential. He told me that, if I carried on that way, I was going to get a life sentence or be shot dead. He said I was worth more than that.

'He encouraged me to go into education. He used to give

me books and newspaper cuttings about business and politics. We would have great discussions on many subjects. His
mind was as sharp as a razor and his knowledge on various
subjects was amazing.

'But he also had a wicked sense of humour. We used to
have one night a week where we would have a smoke and
something to eat, and Charlie would supply entertainment.

'This we called a "loon night". Charlie knew the most
bizarre prisoners with even more bizarre minds. But it was
not just Charlie who could make you laugh.

'His wife Ronnie has a wicked sense of humour. One of the
last parties they attended together was for my wife's birthday.
People flew in from different countries, because Charlie had
always been a globetrotter with his business schemes. One
guy was a high-placed diamond dealer from the Middle East.

'He introduced himself to Ronnie by saying, "I'm A-fief."

'Ronnie, who had had a few drinks, and not really being
a drinker said, "You what?" He said again, "I'm A-fief," to
which Ronnie replied, "I should imagine most of them here
are, but don't go around advertising it." He walked away,
totally confused, and we all thought it was hilarious.

'When Charlie and I met up after leaving prison, he was
really interested in what I was doing and was really
impressed with my set-up and what I have achieved.

'I started up a charity with a few quid with a couple of
other people, and then turned it into a million-pound business. We were fighting for prisoners' rights, with Charlie's
invaluable help.

'In later years, Charlie realised that real wealth was not just in minerals but in family, and his lovely wife, Ronnie, who he loved dearly and who was the jewel in his crown.

'He loved and enjoyed being with all his children and grandchildren, something I saw with my own eyes when they came to visit him.

'The family is the most important thing in life. Crime and prison makes us all bad fathers, and it is our kids and loved ones who pay the price. Charlie realised this and wanted to do something good for all the kids on the street who came from the same background as us. And he was about to do that with us, before he died.

'On the day he died it felt like someone had punched a hole in my chest and ripped my heart out. On that day I lost my dearest friend and a man I loved and respected. I will never be ashamed to say that.

'I'm looking at Charlie's family and friends and know we are all joined in this grief because we are all family, and we will always be there for each other. We will never wash our dirty linen in public or allow the media and those that hate us to divide us, because together we are strong; divided we are weak. Charlie created this family, so let's keep it a family he would be proud of.

'To you, Ronnie, and Charlie's family, I give my condolences, my loyalty, and my love, and will always be there for you.

'Charlie was and still is my dearest friend.'

Rest in peace, Charlie, my best friend of all time.

Life went on. We were waiting on the UK immigration people to grant Ami indefinite leave to stay in this country. Because of an on-going balls-up at the UK Border Agency, we were still waiting when we realised that her passport had nearly run out. We didn't want Ami to be an 'overstayer', so the day before her passport expired we took her to the airport and she flew back to Japan. It wouldn't have been a good idea to have anything bad on her passport.

We had rented an apartment in Japan because of our regular visits and the high cost of hotels, so Ami stayed there with Kai while we tried to sort out her passport over here. If she'd handed over her passport in the UK, waiting for indefinite leave to stay, she wouldn't have been allowed to go back to Japan. If anything had happened to Kai, she wouldn't have been able to travel to see him.

I found – and, sadly, find – the whole situation totally frustrating. Ami helped me to start the Midas charity. She is also a patron of other charities, including a project in Birmingham which looks after young girls who've been on heroin. These girls became prostitutes through drug addiction, but now their lives are being turned round. It is a small project but a highly successful one. It wasn't getting the support it deserved, and when Ami and I both visited the project, we saw what needed to be done. It required backers with higher profiles, so I agreed to join her as a patron. We are both really proud of the work being carried out there.

Ami also worked at a high street bank in the fraud section. At that time I was Chief Executive of Unlock, carrying out many television appearances and advising the government.

I have to tell you that I was unhappy with the way she was treated. Ami has a brilliant brain, and she is always coming up with great ideas. While she worked there, other people nicked those ideas, claiming them as their own when her brainwaves were put into practice.

So you can see why, with all of Ami's qualities, I was pissed off because of the aggravation with her passport. She was working in England and helping charities, and yet having to return to Japan because of the balls-ups and delays with the UK Border Agency.

It is known that Japanese are hard-working, law-abiding and respectful people. My Ami is married to an Englishman. It should be, as previously, that there is an automatic right to citizenship. Nowadays, it is all about money, because you have to go to court to argue your case for citizenship and all that.

Because of the EU, gangsters from Eastern Europe can enter here freely, claim the same rights as a British citizen, and contribute nothing. I have the hump with all of that.

It is common knowledge that I am an out-and-out royalist, passionate about Queen and country. I find it really offensive that the woman I love is not being shown the respect that an Englishman's wife deserves. My marriage is based on love, and not cash.

In the year 2013 I have seen my wife for only two weeks. I haven't seen my son for a year. This is because of Ami's passport saga and her fight for British citizenship. Every time she comes over here, and I go over there, it costs thousands of pounds.

The UK Border Agency and crazy laws are, basically, separating our family. I love my wife and kids more than I love anyone in this world. And yet we are separated by stupid laws laid down by Europe.

How sad is that?

On the Midas front, Paul and I kept going and, at the time of writing, we're working hard to achieve all of our goals.

We believe that you can give someone the best re-education or training in the world, but if they don't want to change they will go back into crime. You have to get them into the mindset that it's better not to be a criminal than to be out there, robbing. Crime is so glamorised that it's not an easy task.

We are trying to include disadvantaged kids, not just ex-offenders or people involved in crime. There are many charities out there working with kids and doing a fine job, but what is really needed is people who've been there, and who understand what is happening. Those people have the street cred that others don't have. That is our powerful asset.

Midas gets right into the people themselves. It's not about 'talking' shops – my charity is about 'doing' shops. We get people into higher education, and work out ways of including training all the way through to finding a job.

If you are a trainer and your training is good, you have to get the people employed at the end of it. It's no good giving ex-offenders bits of paper while they play their part and build up their hopes, but then can't get a job. If you are offering training you must offer hope of a job at the end of it.

I believe that expensive government contracts for rehabilitation are being abused and the money is not going into the right areas: I have watched small concerns in action and have been really impressed. Phoenix Training Services (Midlands) Ltd, Open Book at Goldsmiths College, First Personal in the Midlands and Noor for the Muslim community are prime examples.

Midas is working on a scheme to offer training and apprenticeships, and opportunities to disadvantaged groups. We are encouraging people to take part in sport and arts or enjoy a safe environment to provide relaxation.

We know that the majority of young people today are hopeful, eager to succeed, and more often aware of environmental issues than we adults realise – despite gang culture being hyped up and youths stereotyped by the media. Yet they receive little acknowledgement and encouragement for having good heads on their shoulders, and there are only a handful of opportunities to reward them for their excellence.

I want to give everyone the chance they deserve.

CHAPTER SEVENTEEN

AN OBE FROM THE QUEEN

The letter from the Central Chancery of the Orders of Knighthood told me that I was being considered for an honour. I thought someone had played a trick on me, so I phoned them to make sure it wasn't a hoax!

The Chancery people assured me that it was no hoax and asked me to accept the honour in writing. They said I was receiving the award because I had identified obstacles that needed to be removed so that people – especially the young – could lead positive and crime-free lives. One condition: I could not breathe a word until the list was published on New Year's Day, 2011.

The OBE caught me totally by surprise. I felt like one of those geezers on *This Is Your Life* who have no idea what is happening.

Maybe that shows my age. I used to watch Eamonn Andrews presenting *This Is Your Life*, when people were caught by surprise and their whole life story became public. That was in the early 1960s; Eamonn himself was awarded the CBE.

I was bursting with pride and joy but couldn't tell a soul. I continued with my day job until New Year's Day, sitting in my office under my picture of the Queen: that tradition had continued from my prison cells and my office at Unlock.

A quick look at *Debrett's* told me that I was to be an Officer of the Order of the British Empire. The other alternatives were Commander and Member, so I was pleased to sit in the middle, with my Officer status. I read that the award recognised distinguished service in the arts and sciences, public services outside the Civil Service, and work with charitable welfare organisations.

I scanned the internet and was amazed at the variety of people who'd received the OBE. There were those from the most humble beginnings up to James Bond star, Pierce Brosnan; veteran actor, Eric Sykes; and the comedians, The Goodies. Other recipients ranged from David Beckham to Kylie Minogue. I also noted that John Cleese had turned down a CBE in 1996 because he thought they were silly. I thought his Ministry of Silly Walks sketch was hilarious, but disagreed about his view of the awards.

John Winston Lennon returned his MBE to the Queen in 1969, along with a protest letter. He wasn't happy about Britain's support for America's war in Vietnam and returned the award to make his point.

I saw that Gary Barlow received the OBE. I didn't have his X-Factor and all that, but I must have done something right. At the other end of the scale, I read that a street cleaner had been awarded the British Empire Medal. I liked the sound of that.

And then there was me – a reformed armed robber! I felt a sudden surge of pride as I realised that even an ex-criminal with a dodgy background could turn things around and receive an honour from the Queen.

On 1 January 2011 the announcement was officially made. Now it was no secret, and I could tell my friends and family. I received cards and emails from politicians, judges, police officers and schools where I'd been spreading my anti-crime messages.

On the day, Ami, Kai and my god-daughter Charlotte Baden – daughter of Joe Baden, one of my best friends – booked in to stay in the five-star Royal Horseguards Hotel. That place is the real deal. It is modelled on a French château and has Grade 1 listed building status. The place was originally built as a block of luxury residential departments and it has links to MI5 and MI6.

I woke up on the big day, pinching myself because I was about to head off to Buckingham Palace in my top hat and tails. Professional Japanese dressers kitted Ami out in her kimono. She stood on a little white cloth, as is the tradition, while they dressed her. They worked on her hair and everything very carefully, and I became more and more worried about the time!

And so, on 1 June 2011 – twenty years to the day since my release from prison – we arrived at Buckingham Palace. There was not one cloud in the sky and the palace was bathed in brilliant sunshine. Ami looked absolutely stunning in her national costume. I felt that I looked the part in my top hat and tails.

I saw state rooms the like of which I had never even dreamed of. Priceless paintings were hanging everywhere, while the carpets and furnishings oozed so much class that I was gobsmacked.

We were taken to the most beautiful ballroom I'd seen in my life. I chatted to other recipients, including a soldier who was receiving the Military Cross for bravery. It was a privilege to be in such company. The band played, everyone stood to attention, and the Queen arrived in what appeared to me as a blaze of glory. The place was brimming with colour, palace officials, Yeomen of the Guard and the most ornate decorations I had ever seen.

Names were called, and I was a bit nervous waiting for mine to be read out. I'd thought of what to say, but I was worried that my mind might go blank.

Then an announcement: 'Robert Cummines, to receive the OBE for his work with reformed offenders.'

I marched forward, stood before my Queen and bowed. She pinned the medal on my left breast. I had forgotten what to say. I looked at Her Majesty and said: 'Thank you, ma'am.'

When you meet the Queen, it's as if she is twenty feet tall. I know she is a tiny lady, but she has an aura about her. I could detect strength, kindness, compassion and total authority. It's like being a naughty boy standing in front of your mum and you are waiting to see if you'll be told off. I looked at her and wondered how she could live her life, having to be so perfect all the time.

She helped me to feel calm. I felt so humble. I realised that I respected the monarch so much that I would have happily taken a bullet to save her life.

She had done her research and knew all about me: 'It gives me great pleasure to give you this award. The way you have turned your life around is amazing. You have a very colourful background. You've come a long way. Well done, I'm very pleased for you.'

We had a short chat about my charity, and working with naughty kids and all that. Then we shook hands and I stepped back a couple of paces. You never turn your back on the Queen. I turned to my right, left the hall and walked along to an up-market desk where they placed the OBE in a box for me. Then I returned to the hall, at the back, to join my family.

After the ceremony, we all stood to attention and the Queen left the ballroom, maintaining her incredible level of grace and dignity. After they played 'God Save the Queen' we walked down the enormous hallway to pick up our top hats and everything.

We went outside to have our photographs taken. Although I had the OBE, most of the tourists wanted to take pictures of Ami in her kimono.

I spotted a little boy with his head pushed through the railings. It reminded me of the day my dad took me to

Buckingham Palace to see a ceremony. My dad had pointed to men with tops hats on, and told me: 'See those people – they are the toffs. When you go through that gate with that top hat on, you know you've made it.'

I told the little boy that, one day a long time ago, I had also looked through those railings, full of wonder. I said that one day his dream might become a reality.

I was like a little boy myself as I marvelled at the shiny, gold-coloured medal. It had four arms with three points on each arm. In the centre were King George V and his consort, Queen Mary, surrounded by the words, 'For God and the Empire'. I admired the rose-coloured ribbon with its grey edges.

Our reception at the National Liberal Club was attended by an impressive selection of judges, MPs, senior police officers and ex-villains. Important coppers, who would have been trying to nick me a few years ago, shared stories from the past and enthused about the future for reformed offenders. The judges who would have confronted me in the dock were now eager to learn about my schemes to keep crime off the streets.

Trevor Cox, who runs a training company in Birmingham, brought his young son, William, along. Trevor works with underprivileged people and ex-offenders. William had brought his swimming medal and gave me a little note wishing me good luck. I presented him with a miniature OBE to wear with pride, and said I wanted him to aim for the bigger version.

I want to use William Cox as a role model for young people to focus on. If you want a young person to succeed, you have to invest in that child. William is twelve years of age and goes to a good school that gives its pupils quality education and support. He also has loving parents who play an active role in his education and social life, and show him good family values and manners.

William is a success and has a positive mental attitude. This shows me that, when schools and parents invest in our kids, we can turn out solid citizens for the years ahead. These children are our future and, if we don't invest in them, then we will become the victims in a few years' time.

The day after the ceremony we arrived home, weary but delirious with pride. Halfway through my second cup of tea, the postman arrived with a fancy-looking package. Instead of a warrant for my arrest, it was a Royal Warrant announcing to the rest of the world that I had been awarded the OBE.

The document said that I was an Officer of the British Empire, and it was signed by Her Majesty the Queen. As I read it, I thought about my extraordinary life and the dramatic change in my circumstances: from holding a prison governor hostage to receiving the OBE from the Queen.

My entire life flashed through my head. I thought about those early days, in our ragamuffin gang with Maltese Tony and Silly Billy. I remembered the dramatic day involving 'the stinger'. I recalled when things went right and when they backfired completely.

I pondered for a few moments on all of those years in prison, and how I had realised that crime was not the way forward. I had an image of Charlie Richardson in my mind, telling me to push hard for my education. I smiled as I thought about all the people in the Open University who had recognised my potential, and made sure that I came to the fore.

As I scanned the OBE documents, I said to myself, 'Crime is a mug's game. I am nothing special. If I can turn things around, anyone can. I'm small and wiry, just a tiny guy, and people keep saying there is more fat on a greasy chip. The strength is all inside me.'

I walked over to my desk and flicked through a list of ex-offenders who had gone straight and turned things around. I punched the air when I opened a letter to find out that yet another villain had passed his exams with the promise of a good job.

And, a final message: I'm not going to stop. More and more lives can be turned around. Please, please, kids, stay away from knives and guns and all that, and stay as straight-goers. Look at the difference it has made to my life.

Let's do it!

Leabharlanna Fhine Gall

Balbriggan
Library
Ph: 8704401

AFTERWORD FROM FRED DINENAGE: RIGHT, BOBBY, SAID FRED...

I've been working closely with Fred Dinenage, who used to present World of Sport *in the 1970s. He has worked on news programmes in the South of England for nearly half a century. His latest project,* Murder Casebook, *did what it said on the tin. Fred and I really bounced off each other and became very good friends. Fred wrote a book about the Krays, helped with the Charlie Richardson autobiography and presented countless TV programmes about crime. I asked him to write a section for the end of this book, to get that vital 'outside' view:*

I first heard the name Bobby Cummines some twenty-five years ago in the human hell-hole that masqueraded as the visiting hall at Parkhurst Prison on the Isle of Wight. I was with Reggie Kray, gathering material for *Our Story*, the auto-biography I was writing with Reg and his twin brother, Ron.

We'd reached the point in the twins' story where Reg was awaiting the arrival at Parkhurst of his long-time arch-enemy, Charlie Richardson, from Durham jail.

Parkhurst's governor had objected to Richardson being moved to the prison because he feared violence between the two London gang bosses – violence that could spill over into other parts of the prison. There was, as they say, 'history' between Reg and Charlie.

The Krays had been at loggerheads with Charlie and Eddie Richardson for many years. The Krays controlled the East End of London, while the Richardsons bossed South London. And never the twain should meet – because when they did, there were bloody results.

Before both Reggie and Charlie found themselves banged up – for unrelated offences – there'd been a violent confrontation in March 1966 at a club called Mr Smith's at Rushey Green, Catford. Members of the Kray gang, including a lad called Richard Hart, a cousin of the Krays, were enjoying a drink at the club when they were attacked by members of the Richardson gang, including Eddie Richardson and the infamous 'Mad' Frankie Fraser.

Hart was shot dead, and the Krays vowed revenge. Days later, George Cornell, an enforcer with the Richardson gang, was shot dead at point-blank range by Ronnie Kray in the Blind Beggar public house. Folklore has it that the brutal assassination was carried out to the strains of the Walker Brothers singing 'The Sun Ain't Going to Shine Any More' on the jukebox. It was good night to George, that was for sure.

These two attacks, even more than the battles that had gone on before, ensured that the Krays and the Richardsons wouldn't be on each other's Christmas card lists. Both sets of brothers had vowed revenge, which was precisely why the governor and the warders at Parkhurst were dreading the arrival of one Charles Richardson.

Even Reggie was dreading it. I remember him telling me: 'I thought there would be trouble. I knew everyone expected me to "do" Charlie. But I also knew he could fucking handle himself in a scrap.'

In the end there wasn't a scrap – thanks to another con called Bobby Cummines.

Reggie told me: 'Me and Ron liked Bobby. We met him at the Old Bailey. We were on trial for murder. He was being done for a sawn-off shotgun. And he was only sixteen, for fuck's sake. Both me and Ron thought the little fella had a lot of guts.'

So when Reg and Bobby found themselves banged up at Parkhurst, it was natural that they would become friends. And it was Bobby, in his new role as peacemaker, who brokered a deal between Reg and Charlie. Both would keep a respectful distance between each other – there would be no violence – as neither wanted the authorities to punish them with additional time on top of the already massive sentences they were serving.

As Reggie put it to me: 'Bobby probably had a blade from a pair of shears hidden inside his shirt. Nobody takes any chances inside Parkhurst. It's dog eats dog. It's survival of the fittest. In any event, after that, me and Charlie got along OK. We agreed to not agree, if you see what I mean. There wasn't any bother.'

Ironically, after the peace talks, Bobby probably got

closer to Charlie than he'd even been to Reggie. Charlie, a big reader and a far deeper and more thoughtful and intelligent man than most people ever gave him credit for, found a willing disciple in Bobby. He taught Bobby a lot, and I believe that Bobby will give Charlie Richardson much of the credit for his new path in life.

Charlie Richardson, not a man given to false praise, told me before he died: 'Bobby Cummines is a very intelligent man. If he'd not chosen to be a villain he could have been the fuckin' prime minister! What a waste. Still, it didn't turn out badly for him, did it? Got himself a gong from the Queen. And they'll probably make him a fuckin' Sir one day! I wouldn't put it past the little feller. And good luck to him.'

I first met Bobby Cummines in St Matthew's Church, in Bethnal Green, in the East End. It's the church where all three of the Kray brothers – Reg, Ron and long-suffering older brother, Charlie – had their funeral services. It's also close to their old home in Valence Street. Bobby himself cut quite a striking figure as he entered the church; smaller than I expected, but tough and wiry. He was a fit little bugger, and was always turned out immaculately. On this occasion he wore a beautifully tailored, expensive grey suit, gleaming black shoes, crisp white shirt and a red tie. His hair was neat and tidy. In fact, that's probably the perfect word to sum up Bobby – neat.

With him was a most attractive Japanese lady whom he introduced as his wife, Ami. And with them was their son, a quiet and respectful young lad.

During that cold, crisp but sunny winter Saturday we were filming an hour-long documentary for Sky Television's Crime Investigation Channel on the legacy of the Kray twins.

The day had started in The Carpenter's Arms pub in Cheshire Street – which Reg and Ron had once owned – just a short walk from St Matthew's Church. They bought it for their mum, and as a sort of private club for them and members of the Kray firm. A painting of Reg and Ron still hangs in the bar.

This particular morning, we'd interviewed two of the original Kray firm. Even though it was before ten o'clock in the morning, they'd managed to polish off the contents of a bottle of brandy, but were still relatively coherent as they tottered off to another nearby boozer.

After that, we recorded several links for the programme and then walked the few hundred yards down the road to the church. We did the interview with Bobby Cummines, sitting in a pew near the front of the church. It was, as ever with Bobby, a cracking interview. He told it as it was – as he always does – in those far from halcyon days with Reg Kray and the other inmates of Parkhurst Prison.

He described a daily battle for survival and a regime of fear.

As Bobby put it: 'You had to give respect to everyone. You had to speak to everyone. If you didn't wish some of the prisoners "Good morning", the chances were that they would take it as a slight and come after you.'

Bobby himself was always tooled up with the blade from a pair of shears – just in case. He painted a graphic picture of that time. He gave a full description of Reggie Kray and told how he coped with the prospects of endless years of incarceration. Bobby also described how Reggie dealt with the daily threat of attacks from one of the 'young pretenders', who thought they could make a name for themselves by taking out King Kray.

Reg was always prepared for an attack and always surrounded himself with young thugs who were prepared to die for this underworld legend.

It was a gripping interview. So it was natural that when Sky commissioned a series called *Fred Dinenage's Murder Casebook*, looking back at murder cases from the past, one of our regular contributors would be Bobby Cummines.

Bobby understood the criminal mind and, just as important, he's so articulate that he can explain it to the viewer. We interviewed him a couple of times at Arundel jail in Sussex, which is no longer in use. It was built in 1836 beneath Arundel Town Hall and used to house inmates after they had been convicted in the courtroom upstairs.

The old cells were still there. It's a spooky place, a hotbed for the paranormal – it's claimed it's full of ghosts. I don't know about that. But I do know that Bobby refused to allow himself to be filmed behind bars in one of the cells. Too many bad memories, perhaps?

Later, when we were making a film about Charlie Richardson, we interviewed Bobby on the set of the ITV drama series, *The Bill*. And very realistic that was, too.

Again Bobby was in top form, maybe even more so than

on the Kray documentary, because he'd been very close to Charlie in Parkhurst. Many people say it was Richardson who got Bobby thinking about the future, who persuaded Bobby to read books, and changed the course his life would take. But that's for Bobby himself to describe in this book.

All I would add is that I've interviewed a lot of criminals over the years, but few have impressed me as much as Bobby Cummines. What a pity he chose the path he did so early in his life. Otherwise, as Charlie Richardson said, maybe he could have ended up as our prime minister. Who knows? Maybe one day he will ...

I wouldn't put it past the little fella.

Fred Dinenage, January 2014

BOBBY'S GLOSSARY

I thought it would be interesting to write down some of the words and phrases used by firms in London in the 1970s. You will see examples in the book, although I have tried to explain them where possible.

A bit of bird or a stretch: jail sentence

A bit of work: criminal activity

A blade: knife or a razor

A blag: armed robbery

A bullseye: £50

A diamond: a solid person with the highest possible reputation

A drink: giving someone money

A face: well-known villain

A fixer: peacemaker

A grand: £1,000

A piece: handgun

A ruck: a fight

A score: £20

A ton: £100

Apples and pears: stairs

Bag man: one who takes the bag from a security man or takes money from the tills

Barnet: hair

Bent gear: stolen goods

Bit of tom: jewellery

Boat race: face

Brown bread: dead

Bung: bribe

Chokey or block: solitary confinement

Cleaning money: money laundering

Cockle: £10

Contract: a death sentence

Creeper: burglar

Deps: depositions of a trial

Dog and bone: telephone

Educate: teach or punish

Ghosted: removal of disruptive prisoner to another jail

Going copper, cat's arse or grass: police informant

Going up the steps: going to the Old Bailey

Heavy game: crimes involving violence or death

Jam jar: car

Jekyll and Hyde: snide or fake

Jump up: stealing from the backs of lorries

Kiss the Axminster: get on the floor

Kneecapping: shooting someone in the legs

Long firm: organised fraud

Mule: drug smuggler

Nanny goat: coat

Nonce: sex offender

On the firm: part of a crime family

On your toes: on the run

Pavement man: one who controls the street

Peter: prison cell or a safe

Plates of meat: feet

Pop one in the ceiling: shotgun fired at the ceiling

Pushing up daises: person is buried

Rat: a person without honour

Safe house: where you meet before the robbery and go back
  afterwards

Saucepan lids: the kids

Sawn-off: cut-down shotgun

Screws: prison officers

Snide gear: counterfeit goods

Spiller: illegal drinking and gambling club

Stinger: shotgun cartridge with buckshot taken out and
  rock salt put in

Strong arm: demanding money with menaces

Sweeney: police's heavy mob

Thrupenny bits: tits

Tool merchant: someone who uses weapons or supplies them

Trouble and strife: wife

Well recommended: someone from another firm who comes
  on to your firm

Whacked: killed

Wheel man: driver for villains

BOBBY'S POEMS

I hope you enjoyed my poem, 'The one who locked my door'.
Here are a few others, written in solitary confinement:

TONGUE IN CHEEK

Now I don't mind this solitary
Because my thoughts, like birds, take flight
I can go just where I choose
You can never deny me that right

In my mind I have travelled
Even to where you are
Hovering high above you
And you thought me just a star

I think they have begun to realise
Solitary is no punishment to me
As I sit in the middle of this bare cell
And smile back at them happily

I see the havoc in their minds
If only they really knew
I am sure they would sit down with me
And come and travel too

FOR YOU

I wish that for a day you could be me
See the world through my eyes
Then you could see how I now see
And my pain you would realise

You would hear the voice of my soul
Give comfort to those in pain
You will understand I judge no man
For nobody is without blame

You will understand how deep I feel
You will know, too, the depths of my love
For all the things that move upon this earth
And the birds that fly above

But in a way I am glad you're not me
That you cannot feel as I do
For each of us is a priceless jewel
Which means you are priceless too

LOVE'S POWER

I have killed
It meant nothing to me
I have lived like a king
It meant nothing to me

I have been tortured
It meant nothing to me
I have dared myself to dream
It meant nothing to me

I have made my own philosophy
It meant nothing to me
I have made violence my voice
It meant nothing to me

I have been a god
It meant nothing to me
I fell in love
It made me mortal

A PRISON SUICIDE

What kind of perverse, sick system
Can make a man turn to the rope?
What kind of brutal apathy
Can take away all hope?

What frame of mind were you in?
That your friends you could not tell?
What kind of suffering did you feel
That made your life a hell?

What was your final thought, my friend
That you had upon this Earth?
The thought that said 'End it all'
And return to the place before birth

What was it that made your soul
Decide it wanted to be free?
It was the penal code devised by man
That you suffered along with me

PAPER TIGERS

He struts along this cell block
He thinks he's a chap
He is easily recognised
He talks mostly crap

He will tell you he's a gangster
But there's no need for alarm
He is only a paper tiger
Says a red band on his arm

He is an empty vessel
That makes so much noise
But please don't disillusion him
He is one of the boys

He deludes himself in thinking
He's the cock of the walk
But they've given him a red band
To prove he's only talk.

[Note: A prisoner who was trusted by staff was known as a
'trustee' and wore a red band. They could walk around the prison
unescorted. They were not trusted by the other prisoners!]

THOSE WHO STUDY LAW

A wig, a gown, a bible, a pen
These are the tools of your trade
And you quote strange words from your dusty books
A list of laws men have made

You choose your words so carefully
So they cannot be twisted by knaves
For you are duty bound to uphold the laws
They dictate how men behave

But justice and laws are two strange things
And they do not always agree
And it is at such time that a jury
Must decide what the verdict must be

It is at such times we pray to God
That their verdict will be correct
Because if it's wrong, no matter which way
Then the laws are in neglect.

THAT HAPPY LITTLE BIRD

A bird flew around my window
Singing songs no man had heard
Such happiness he gave me
That happy little bird

He sang me songs of freedom
Freedom no human knew
The current of the winds of time
On which my little friend flew

He told me all life's secrets
As I fed him milk and bread
Of all the heroes of mythology
Who for a thousand years lay dead

Walking around the yard today
What I saw brought a tear to my eye
Some prison cat had killed that bird
No more would he sail the sky

THE SIMPLE LIFE

I don't want your big fancy cars
Or your modern washing machines
When the flowing rivers are just as good
And keep my clothes twice as clean

I don't want a bank account
To hide away my loot
All the money I really need
I can hide in my boot

I don't want to move mountains
Jut to gain a slap on the back
Along with all the worry it brings
That causes a heart attack

I don't want status symbols
Or a badge of authority
As long as I know I'm an honest man
That's all that matters to me

What I would like is to be a free man
To go just where I please
And hear the songs of the birds
The whisper of the breeze

HYPOCRISY

People saying words they don't mean
Expressing emotions they don't feel
They're singing songs of brotherly love
But wishing they could kill

What a crazy world we live in
This whole world's gone insane
War is no justification
Politicians won't take the blame

The children we watch burning
They're using napalm bombs
On Sundays they're in churches
Singing gospel songs

All dressed in garbs of finest silk
Jewels set in purest gold
A hungry child stretches out its hand
To a heart it knows is cold.

JUDAS

When I was free and victorious
You loved and praised my name
But you were nowhere to be found
When the roar of the battle came

You watched me battle on alone
Without a shield or sword
You saw them whip and crucify me
And never said a word

Though guards and chains restrained me
I fought every inch of the way
You saw the sentence they gave me
Not a comforting word did you say

These arms that once held you
The warmth of loving and giving
You watched as they placed me in this tomb
Buried whilst still living

SHORT-TERM PRISONER

I watch you walk this cell block
And, young man, I feel your pain
I relate to you so easily
Because I once felt the same

But I hope you never see the real horrors
That I have seen in this cage
The total lack of humanity
That brutalise and outrage

You think you have a problem
But, my friend, ours are so small
Compared to those serving life
Never to see beyond the wall

So don't let your pain cripple you
Open up your eyes and see
That you have no real problem
Because, one day at least, you'll be free

THE BATTLE WITHIN MYSELF

I have fought many a strange battle
On many a foreign shore
Followed many strange philosophies
Entered many a strange door

Seen the faces of life's monsters
The faces of lust and greed
Have seen the fantasies within this dream
That cater for most men's needs

Yet still searching for the truth
The truth that might be a lie
Looking at the essence of life
And slowly seeing it die

Accumulating great pleasures
Trying to assess true wealth
Fighting the hardest battle of my life
The battle within myself

A WARRIOR KNOWS ALL THESE THINGS

No place to rest this weary soul
No soft warm feathered bed
No emotions to show in this cold war
Just battles that waited ahead

There are many ways to kill a man
A Judas kiss or a cold steel blade
A warrior knows all these things
But battles on, unafraid

The sword of love is the most ruthless tool
That mankind has ever used
For when that sword has been drawn
Then love itself is abused

And when the war has come to an end
We each tally up the score
And bind our wounds and walk away
Because love exists no more

BOARD OF VISITORS

They say they're there to protect prisoners
Follow up prisoners' complaints
As they take away your remission
This board of unholy Saints

They smile and listen to your plight
But to them you're just lowlife
They couldn't give a damn for your children
Even less for your struggling wife

They are an android type of people
Born of a brutal machine
They don't care about abused prisoners
As long as the paperwork's clean

They sit in judgement on kangaroo courts
They crucify everyone
Yet they tell you they protect our rights
But how can they – when we have none?

MY MOTHER

She's always there when she's needed
And that's always been the case
She's always a source of comfort
A warm and gentle face

She's always understanding
Stands by me through thick and thin
She can never see the wrong in me
I am always free from sin

She has a heart of pure gold
She would give you her last shilling
If ever anybody needed help
She would be there, ever willing

She never makes a lot of fuss
She believes we should help one another
And I'm so proud to be able to say
This beautiful soul is my mother

CONTRARY TO APPEARANCE

You think of me as a chained man
Restrained by locks and bars
A man denied all privileges
Such as gazing at the stars

You think of me as a broken man
Locked securely in a cell
Being tormented by life's demons
That dwell in this living hell

But never judge a book by its cover
Gaze deeply into my eyes
For they are the mirrors of my soul
And by them you will realise

That all of us are prisoners
You as well as me
And freedom is a state of mind
And it is I who am truly free

TIME

Time for loving
Time for tears
Weeks turn to months
Months turn to years

Time for reflections
Time to forget
The happiness and laughter
The sadness and regret

That youthful beauty
Now withered with age
Wrinkles of time
We count with rage

Time is a thief
A destroyer of the dream
As it ticks off the days
That is life's theme

HE PEDDLES DREAMS

He peddles dreams
He peddles hope
He deals in substances
Labelled dope

He deals in illusions
Is the father of lies
He will take your money
Ignore your cries

He talks of philosophies
He thinks he's hip
He sings of no possessions
Whilst pocketing the blue chip

He will sell to the wealthy
He will sell to the bum
He will peddle to children
He really is scum

MY TRUTH IS MY POETRY

An armour of golden sunlight
To cover my naked skin
The power not created by men of war
But by the love I feel within

My legions are those visionary men
Who speak through the poem's verse
Men who need no shield or sword
When their truth inflicts wounds far worse

For the poem is the voice of God
Spoken through the soul
And through the words of such poetry
He shows the picture as a whole

My kingdom is my vision
My jewels, flowers of the Earth
My truth is in my poetry
That truth gave my poetry birth

A MESSAGE FROM THE OPEN UNIVERSITY

Bobby's story is the epitome of all we hope for with every one of the offenders we work with. We are particularly proud of the fact that many students continue their studies when they have served their term and are released into the community. Our work with the Prisoners' Education Trust, which provides learning opportunities for offenders and awards grants to prisoners to fund distance learning modules, demonstrates the impact that access to educational opportunities can have.

Of the prisoners who are awarded grants, only around one quarter go on to re-offend, compared to an average re-offending rate of around 65 per cent for all prisoners. Considering the personal challenges facing these prisoners upon their release, this is a compelling and outstanding achievement.

Now we have about 1,700 students on more than 200 courses across all of the university's faculties in approximately 150 prisons (covering all security categories) in the UK and Ireland.

During this entire forty-year history, the university has constantly refined and redeveloped the delivery of its Offender Learning Programme to meet the unique challenges and constraints posed by working with offenders in prison and secure units and ensure that our offering to them remains high quality, consistent, safe and accessible.

And not only does the university's work in prisons demonstrate our commitment to widening participation wherever and however we can, but, led by our Centre for Inclusion and Collaborative Partnerships, it also enables us to trial and innovate new methods of face-to-face support and virtual delivery that might potentially help a much wider pool of disadvantaged students. Nationally, we have an average of more than 600 offender learners each year undertaking an access module, and during any one presentation the Centre might have students in around 80 prisons. We aim to overcome the negative reinforcements of an offender's surroundings to help make them aware of the possibility of a very different future, as we work with them to provide the means that could make this a reality.

I myself recently had the opportunity to attend a degree ceremony in a prison. As many people will know, an Open University degree ceremony is always an inspiring occasion, but this one was particularly moving. The pride in the room was even more palpable than usual – from his family, his friends and the prison staff present, including the governor – at the efforts of this man to put his previous life behind him and complete what is an enormous achievement in any circumstances.

Lucian J. Hudson, Director of Communications, 2014

AUTHOR'S NOTE

When I go around the schools, I spread this message: In the 1960s and 1970s everyone went to college and university for free, but we robbed today's young people of the same privileges. We were all greedy bastards, looking out for ourselves and not their futures.

We moan that our kids don't respect us. Why should they? We didn't respect them. We didn't invest in their futures, and make them leave college and university with massive debts. We robbed their money boxes.

Let's make sure that they have a proper education and help them to choose the right path in life. I took a long time to find that path; let's ensure that our children don't make my mistakes.

Please accept my heartfelt thanks to everyone who has written to me and given their support over so many years. Your backing meant everything to me. Everything.

CHONTAE ÁTHA CLIATH THEAS